Thomas N. Hackney

The ETi Grail

BALBOA.
PRESS

A DIVISION OF HAY HOUSE

ISBN: 978-1-4525-5511-9 (sc)
ISBN: 978-1-4525-5512-6 (e)
ISBN: 978-1-4525-5513-3 (hc)

Library of Congress Control Number: 2012912859

Balboa Press books may be ordered through booksellers or by contacting:

Balboa Press
A Division of Hay House
1663 Liberty Drive
Bloomington, IN 47403
www.balboapress.com
1-(877) 407-4847

Because of the dynamic nature of the Internet, any web addresses or links contained in this book may have changed since publication and may no longer be valid. The views expressed in this work are solely those of the author and do not necessarily reflect the views of the publisher, and the publisher hereby disclaims any responsibility for them.

The author of this book does not dispense medical advice or prescribe the use of any technique as a form of treatment for physical, emotional, or medical problems without the advice of a physician, either directly or indirectly. The intent of the author is only to offer information of a general nature to help you in your quest for emotional and spiritual well-being. In the event you use any of the information in this book for yourself, which is your constitutional right, the author and the publisher assume no responsibility for your actions.

Any people depicted in stock imagery provided by Thinkstock are models, and such images are being used for illustrative purposes only.
Certain stock imagery © Thinkstock.

Printed in the United States of America

Balboa Press rev. date: 08/30/12

The ETi Grail

Preface

Hello, my name is Thomas Nelson Hackney, private advocate, investigator, lost soul. I look for extraterrestrials in the damnedest places. Hop into my cab and I promise you a lively ride, but hire me only if you want the truth, or maybe to see evolution in action. You see, I've been looking for that significant "other" for a long time. One day I actually found it!

An extraterrestrial communication was not exactly what scientists at NASA were looking for at the time. Yet, paradoxically, ET-produced "signals" were the thing, the *very* thing, scientists around the world were looking for -- at the time, you see. From this apparent discrepancy I will prove, beyond a shadow of a sapient doubt, that a highly advanced, non-human intelligence *exists!*

Here is a brief but reasonably comprehensive account of some fairly miraculous events, mostly in the order in which they happened. Yet miracles are rare, and they often have rational explanations. These events are no different. No-one disputes they happened, but it was through these events that an indirect communication *was* dispatched to the inhabitants of Earth. The main purpose of this book is to elucidate that communication.

This may sound like nothing new to some, but the sad and stubborn truth of the matter is there has *never* been any hard, scientifically verified, or museum-quality evidence for the existence of intelligent extra-solar life. Now there is.

It's been just about twenty years at this writing since I saw on my television screen the *first* event that set up this ETi communication. Does this make it ancient history? I hardly think so. If it were needed -- and someone "out there" seems to think it *was* needed -- this seems like more than enough time to soften any impact of news of this magnitude. As far as documentation is concerned, the points recalled in this book are literally rock solid. What's more, most of it is readily available on the worldwide web.

Yes, the subject matter of this book is extraterrestrials (I'm sorry about this, but there's just no way around it), but not in any sense you've ever heard of. Some people I have known say they see aliens all the time, or what they think are their spacecraft, anyway. I seriously doubt this. Let me make something clear right now; *I do not flock with the UFO crowd.* The alien cars (if they exist) hold no interest for me, and never have. But I do believe extraterrestrials exist; in fact, I am sure they do. So step on up and make yourself comfortable, or as comfortable as you can; and by all means, fasten your seat belt, because Kansas is going bye-bye.

Give me solid interworld *communication*, anytime. This is what I chronicle in this book. I call it the real thing. I call it *The ETI Grail.*

There is one simple Divinity found in all things, once fecund nature, preserving mother of the universe in so far as she diversely communicates herself, casts her light into diverse subjects, and assumes various names.

- Giordano Bruno

One
Infinite Worlds

**Father Giordano Bruno
(1548-1600) - Father of
the modern universe**

Agreat awakening is taking place, has been taking place for almost six-hundred years. It began with the Renaissance of the Middle Ages, which was marked by a rebirth in human thinking, self-expression and learning. It led directly to what historians call the Age of Reason and Enlightenment. This awakening is still opening eyes today because the search for new and rationally arrived at truth remains the driving force and indispensable activity of our times.

One of the more important thinkers of the early renaissance was Giordano Bruno, a 16th century Dominican Catholic priest-philosopher from Naples.

Father Giordano, as he was known, read a lot of books, not all of them approved books, which made him one of the most widely read and learned men of his time. He also wrote a lot of books, more than twenty by most accounts, though many of them seem forgotten or lost today. Bruno was able to retain everything that he read. He was renowned in his time for possessing one of the most amazing memories in his day, a skill which in the 16th century was considered very much the thing. King Henri III of France once asked him to personally explain his memory techniques, which involved the use of geometric symbols, figures, circles and tables.

But what made Bruno really special was his ability or predisposition to integrate and ultimately reformulate information in new and startling ways. This he did, most notably, with Nicolaus Copernicus's revolutionary and suppressed book, <u>De revolutionibus orbium coelestium</u> (On the Revolutions of the Celestial Spheres). The book, first printed in 1543 in Nuremberg, offered evidence that the Earth went around the Sun, and not vice versa, as had been thought.

Bruno used his eyes and brain to put this crucial bit of cosmological information into its proper perspective. It must have happened one night when he looked up at a star-studded night sky and had one of the great *Eureka!* moments ever. What an original mind like his realized was that the stars were nothing less than *Suns*, shining from very, very far away. Indeed, this was why they appeared so small, why they merely twinkled rather than blazed like the Sun.

The idea of infinity had always fascinated and mystified Bruno. Because he was both a "God-intoxicated man" and an accomplished mathematician (in 1589 Galileo beat him out for the Mathematics Chair at the University of Pisa), the concept was bound to confront and compel him, for it was something both real and quite beyond man's grasp. For Bruno this was what distinguished man from God, because in a sense God was the spiritual embodiment of infinity. Only an infinite universe was consonant with the infinite creative power of God, and one of the best ways to know the deity was through the study of mathematics and nature.

Bruno's fascination with infinity and the natural world led him to another epiphany: like God, the universe *had* to be infinite! From this simple and logical insight, the universe cascaded before him. The universe was *not* divided into 55 concentric "crystalline spheres" as the pagan Aristotle had posited nearly two-thousand years earlier. Although the Church had made Aristotle's scheme Catholic doctrine well before his time, Bruno was not deterred. He believed strongly in the primacy of the intellect, and particularly in the new science of clear observation. He understood only too well that certain aspects of nature could not be merely agreed upon by some high church council and thus forever be considered the truth. The Church made much of the spiritual world and impugned the natural world, so why should the Church know all the right answers about the natural world if this wasn't its true province?

For the Church, the physical world was illusory and unimportant, but in Bruno's world, the natural and spiritual worlds were one, and God generously revealed himself to man through the structure and processes of nature. Unfortunately for Bruno, the Church wasn't having any, certainly not from an upstart who had been suspected of heresy even during his Dominican training days. Besides, Church doctrine was written in stone, and by challenging the infallibility of the Holy See, Bruno went too far.

Bruno was not a very practical man, but more than the other Italian philosophers who were his contemporaries, he was a prime mover and advocate of science, and for the, then, sinful notion of independent thought.

Bruno's eyes and brain told him things that put him literally hundreds of years ahead of Galileo and the rest of the intellectuals of his time. He was the first to realize that since the universe consisted of an infinite number of Suns, then there would also have to be an infinite number of *planets* revolving around these Suns. Having studied Copernicus's highly suppressed book, he could now comprehend how the universe was organized. An infinite number of planets meant an

3

infinite number of intelligent beings living on those planets *(big fat Eureka!)*, for why would God go to all the trouble of creating so many planets if not to populate them?

While these ideas were mostly laughed off by his contemporaries, Bruno became the first human being to correctly describe the basic size, structure *and* potential of the universe. His cosmic view remains essentially the same model of the cosmos we ascribe to today.

Because Bruno deplored dogma, much of which he held was arbitrary or even stupid, he was ex-communicated three different times by three different churches -- first by the Catholic Church, then by the Calvinist Church, and last by the Lutherans. He converted to each denomination in turn, but his anti-authoritarian and fecund mind always managed to get him kicked out of whichever order he ascribed to. His was a modern mind trapped in a supernatural world, though his scholarly and prescient books, the bootleg literature of his day, were read by all the right people of his day -- kings, queens, and noted intellectuals, like the illustrious Sir Philip Sidney and Robert Dudley, the earl of Leicester.

Well, this made the Church mad. This renegade itinerant friar was an embarrassment, his ideas dangerous. All this business about intellectual and philosophical freedom was a bitter pill for the Church to have to endure. Things finally caught up with him in 1593 after he had been lulled back to Italy to teach his memory system to a Venetian nobleman. He was quickly captured and imprisoned by the Holy Inquisition, only to be burned at the stake in Rome seven years later on February 17, 1600 as "an impertinent and pertinaceous heretic."

He famously told his executioners in 1600, "You perhaps tremble more in pronouncing the sentence than I in receiving it." Unlike Galileo a few decades later, Bruno held tenaciously to his beliefs, even to the end. He became not only a martyr for intellectual and *philosophical liberty* (he coined the phrase) but a martyr for the infinite God, as well.

Galileo had been one of those who laughed off Bruno's theory of an infinite universe of suns and their revolving planets, calling it "wild and unprovable." Galileo later retracted many of his own scientifically posited beliefs, if only to save his own skin at the not-so-merciful hands of the Catholic Church and its torture department, the Holy Inquisition. On the other hand, by refusing to recant his cosmological beliefs, even under torture, Bruno had the greater impact on history. While Galileo became the "father of modern science" (no mean tribute), Bruno became *a* father of philosophical liberty, as well as *the* father of the modern universe, though he is generally not given this sort of credit. In this book, we will accord him the credit he deserves because, for one thing, his observational approach is the crucial one we must use to prove what Bruno only logically postulated.

In late 1992, the Catholic Church officially pardoned Galileo for his cosmological views. Bruno's cosmological revelations, on the other hand, continue to stick in its throat, even as they compel and show us how to search for an Other.

In his book <u>De la Causa, principio et uno, (On Cause, Principle, and Unity)</u> we find some prophetic phrases:

> *"This entire globe, this star, not being subject to death, and dissolution and annihilation being impossible anywhere in Nature, from time to time renews itself by changing and altering all its parts. There is no absolute up or down, as Aristotle taught; no absolute position in space; but the position of a body is relative to that of other bodies. Everywhere there is incessant relative change in position throughout the universe, and the observer is always at the center of things."*

While we're at it, here is another little gem that still speaks to us today.

> *It is proof of a base and low mind for one to wish to think with the masses or majority, merely because the majority is the*

> *majority. Truth does not change because it is, or is not, believed by a majority of the people.*

Bruno's notions about the universe proved to be not so "wild and unprovable" at all, but, rather, quite accurate. Although this took a few hundred years to finally make itself apparent, his idea that mankind was not alone in the universe, that neither the Earth nor the Sun was the center of everything, nor even particularly special in the grand scheme of things, has become a trademark of modern cosmological thinking.

The Other

For as long as humans have huddled around the relative safety of cook fires, there must have come the odd moment when that certain kind of question was asked: what in the heck is going on here? What *is* this place, this solid ground and moving sky? What is existence? The cooked food and safety that our fires afforded us gave ample opportunity to direct our large and growing brains to thinking about the things we sensed around us. It was noted, for example, that objects far away on the plain appear small, or even tiny as ants, but that the closer they approached the larger they grew. In fact, there was some sort relationship there, something one could count on, something that was always true. It was also something that could mean the difference between life and death on the plain.

At some point people began to ask, whence came this place? How did the universe and everything in it get here? While fascinating to some, they are questions for which there are no real answers, even today. Although some believe they know where the universe came from and how it all started, the hard truth is no one really knows. It is easy to put everything in a box and call it God or "The Big Bang", but these explanations cannot really satisfy the seriously inquiring mind. Even if God did create the universe from nothing, or some "infinitely dense" cosmic nut did explode to create the universe and time, these attributions do nothing to elucidate *how* God created the universe, or where the original nut came from. In other words, where did the first *something* come from? "Always was and always will be" is not an answer. Besides, what does "always" and "forever" mean? Try as we might, our human minds are just not equipped to wrap themselves around the concepts. So we are essentially bereft of the deep answers, find ourselves in basically the same boat we were in a hundred-thousand years ago: no "Others" to touch or hold, and no enduring answers to the really big questions, not one.

One's world view, whether it be yours or mine or that of a great philosopher, may be thought of as many pieces of a jig-saw puzzle. The pieces are scattered everywhere in time and space. Some date back to earliest childhood, others draw from earliest antiquity, while others are now in the process of being born. Often they have baffling shapes. Nonetheless, each one of us during the course of his or her life attempts to fit the pieces together so that they will form a coherent picture, one that makes it possible for us to confidently navigate the world with something other than doe-in-the-headlights eyes. History is the story of how different people at different times have woven different patterns and solutions to the puzzle. In one significant corner of the puzzle is a large and somewhat diaphonous piece that follows our perennial search for some fully sentient Other. We have given this hypothetical entity many names over the millenia-- Apollo, Jehovah, Satan, Big Foot, Amaterasu (Japan), Anubis (ancient Egypt), to name a tiny few. We have created entire categories and sub-categories in which to organize and place these sentient or magical creatures -- elves, aliens, demons, spirits, fae, gnomes, angels, and so on.

This writing tells of a man's journey to discovering just such an entity and being. The presumption that this entity is of the flesh-and-blood *extraterrestrial* kind is backed up by multiple levels of evidence, but one shouldn't always be too sure about such things. In any case, the entity or entities reveal themselves through events of their own making, events so conspicuous and unique that humans were able to document them in every way that events *can* be documented. From this I infer that the entity or entities in question now wish to make their co-existence known to us, even if this was undertaken in a way certain federally commissioned investigators did not want or expect.

No one doubts that the events in question happened; two of them can easily be placed among the most fully documented events of their kind in history. What remains in some doubt, however, is their cause, for which only two possibilities exist. The main ambition of this book is to show why these *particular* related events could not have been blind accidents of nature, but had to be intelligently caused.

Before they occurred, nothing had ever been found or seen which everyone in the world could point to and say, here is proof positive of an Other's physical existence. Support for this statement comes in the form of a large number of clear, precise, and *articulate* event details, details that accrue to a critical mass of proof for the proposition that a communication has taken place.

Many are content to take other peoples' word for the existence of a signifcant Other. Judeo-Christian religious people believe Moses *did* return from a mountain with tablets personally inscribed by God. Non-Judeo-Christian religious people tend not to take Moses at his word on this. How many people believe what a UFO abductee claims, that he or she has had personal contact with a group of bland, stick-figure aliens who performed wierd medical procedures on them? Not a great many, I would guess. But the hard cold facts in *this* case are plain and easy to find or look up. I do not need to ask the reader to take my word for anything. I only ask that he or she seriously consider the facts as variously recorded in photographs, films, journalistic accounts, and meticulous scientific studies.

I realize that the very mention of extraterrestrials, or of sentient Others of any kind, is enough to cause many to ignore anything else proclaimed along such lines. Given the extraordinary number of these claims made in a typical month, this is quite understandable. The evidence presented in this book, however, stands alone and apart from such claims for a number of reasons. First, the objects involved in the communications were *identified*, not unidentified. The "U" in UFO stands for unidentified, whereas the events here involved IFOs (Identified Flying Objects). Two of the objects were so well identified, in fact, that their names have been written large in both history books *and* the scientific literature. For another thing, the events described in this book have never happened before, which is to say, they were all unprecedented in some way. But, by far the most important reason these events were different from anything cited previously is that they contained what appears to be an extraterrestrial communication. Although this communication was of an unusual nature and style, it was nevertheless replete with ideas, dates, predictions, mathematical symmetry, historical and cultural references, context, symbolism, analogies, antithesis, sarcasm, and warnings.

The question will still often arise: why can't a nonhuman entity just come out in the open and say, in English, "Hello, glad to meet you", so that anyone, or almost anyone, can be well satisfied? This book reveals how one or more nonhuman entities came quite close to doing just that. But there was a catch, alas! There will be no holding or *be*holding the communicant, not in this round. Nor will there be a public disclosure of phenotype (physical appearance), planet of origin, or anything else of potential strategic value to generals. *Because* there is no physical "alien" for anyone to exploit or focus his attention on, many will therefore throw out the data as useless and irrelevant. This I find a shame. But pretty much everything else in terms of context, motivation and timing that could be given was given.

I think it behooves us to take good look at this possible ET overture from ETi (as I shall refer to he/she/it/them -- pronounced ĕtty). Maybe even a very close look is in order. I will not be able in this short book to explore all the social, scientific and political ramifications of this phenomenologically perceived communication, but I will cover what I think are the most important bases.

"The heart has its reasons which reason does not know."

-- Blaise Pascal

Two
NASA searches for ETI

The perennial human search for another - *any* other - entered a new phase on October 12, 1992, with the commencement of a ten-year NASA project to search for extraterrestrials. Traditionally known as SETI (Search for Extra-Terrestrial Intelligence), the technical name given the federal project was the High Resolution Microwave Survey (HRMS). The "New York Times" called it "The first comprehensive high technology search for evidence of intelligent life elsewhere in the universe" (10/11/92).

With the flip of a switch, a new epoch in man's socio-cosmic life began. That day was Monday, the 500th Columbus Day. Columbus discovered a new world on October 12, 1492, so why shouldn't NASA discover one exactly 500 years later? Of course!

Although the search for ETI (Extra-Terrestrial Intelligence) had already been attempted on several dozen previous occasions, none of these could compare with what would now be accomplished in a single minute. The "New York Daily News" quoted John Billingham of the Ames Research Center, one of the project's main architects, as saying, "In the first few minutes, more searching will be accomplished than in all previous searches *combined*." HRMS was, indeed, *orders* of magnitude more efficient at collecting and analyzing radio-wave signals from space than any previous SETI (Search for Extra-Terrestrial Intelligence) project before it.

HRMS peered far and wide into space in search of *non*-random, intelligently produced, microwave signals. Utilizing football field-sized radio-telescopes located around the globe (the largest was more than three football fields in diameter), the human race, in effect, stood on the shores of a cosmic ocean searching for intelligent life "out there."

The range of the search was a few hundred light-years. In galactic terms, this was not a huge distance, but the ETI investigators at the Ames Research Center and Jet Propulsion Laboratory had reason for some optimism. The prevailing scientific theory has it that the galaxy *could* be fairly teeming with intelligent life. So the possibility of finding signs of this life, even within a modest range, might almost be considered good.

The High Resolution Microwave Survey was conducted in two parts over a range of radio frequencies between 1,000 megahertz and

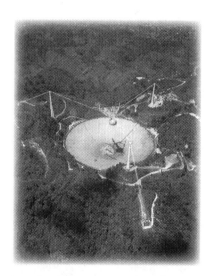

10,000 megahertz, a range considered to be the most likely band for interstellar radio communications. Lower frequencies become easily contaminated by galactic noise, whereas higher frequencies are mostly absorbed by the earth's atmosphere. One of these parts, the Targeted Search, was designed to intensely probe up to 1,000 sun-like stars within 100 light-years of Earth. It's primary tool for accomplishing this was the 1,000 foot radio-telescope located in Arecibo, Puerto Rico, the largest radio-astronomy dish antenna on the planet. Utilizing innovative integrated circuitry and new digital techniques specially developed for the project,

Arecibo Observatory, the 305 meter radio telescope near the city of Arecibo, Puerto Rico is the largest radio telescope on Earth. The facility was used by NASA's Ames Research Center to conduct the High Resolution Microwave Survey, beginning October 12, 1992.

Arecibo was capable of listening to 14 million channels simultaneously in the radio band between 1,000 and 3,000 megahertz. Because Arecibo was teamed up with the radio-telescope at the National Radio and Astronomy Observatory (NRAO) in West Virginia, the Parkes Observatory in Australia, and others around the globe, this would allow the ETI investigators to maintain a continuous 24-hour vigil of targets of interest in the sky.

The second phase of the project, called "All Sky", was directed by the Jet Propulsion Laboratory (JPL) in Pasadena, California. It surveyed deeper into space but with a less focused intensity. All Sky utilized the Deep Space Network in Goldstone, California as it searched the full microwave spectrum up to 10,000 megahertz. All Sky also hooked up with other radio-telescopes around the world, including those in Russia, Argentina, and India. HRMS was very much a global effort.

The idea that NASA was effectively attempting to eavesdrop on another planetary civilization's transmissions was, of course, not considered. HRMS was pure research, after all, so any civilizations discovered via this research shouldn't really mind too much, should they? When Christopher Columbus reached out in 1492, he was testing an ambitious hypothesis, too, namely, that the earth is round. Although the conclusion had already been assumed by the scholars of the time, the final proof would be provided by sailing due West from Spain and arriving in the East Indies from the East. No one figured on there being an entire unknown continent in between. Columbus never knew what he had discovered for as long as he lived, because like everyone else he always assumed that he had found some unknown region in the East Indies.

Much of any scientific or SETI reasoning behind NASA's optimism for the prospect of actually discovering intelligently made signals in space came from what's known as *Drake's equation*. This highly theoretical equation attempts to estimate the number of ET-inhabited planets in the Milky Way galaxy, as follows:.

$$N = R^* \times fp \times ne \times f_\ell \times fi \times fc \times L$$

where:

N = the number of civilizations in our galaxy with which communication might be possible;

and

R^* = the average rate of star formation per year in our galaxy

f_p = the fraction of those stars that have planets

n_e = the average number of planets that can potentially support life per star that has planets

f_ℓ = the fraction of the above that actually go on to develop life at some point

f_i = the fraction of the above that actually go on to develop intelligent life

f_c = the fraction of civilizations that develop a technology that releases detectable signs of their existence into space

L = the length of time for which such civilizations release detectable signals into space

In 1960, Dr. Frank Drake conducted the first search for extraterrestrial radio signals at the National Radio and Astronomy Observatory (NRAO) in Green Bank, West Virginia. Soon after, the National Academy of Sciences asked Drake to convene a meeting on detecting extraterrestrial intelligence in space, which formally established SETI as a scientific discipline. The meeting, held at the Green Bank facility in 1961, produced the equation that bears his name.

What is interesting about Drake's equation is the weight it puts on the inability of technological civilizations to avoid self-destruction. Drake suggested that judging from what is known about life formation on Earth, a large number of extraterrestrial civilizations *should* exist, but the lack of such evidence (the Fermi paradox) suggests that technological races tend to disappear rather quickly.

The American astronomer and popular science writer, Carl Sagan, basically concurred with this view since he contended that all of the terms in Drake's equation except one have relatively high values, that the determining factor in whether there are large or small numbers of extraterrestrial civilizations is their lifetime, or ability to avoid self-destruction. But where is the evidence to support this proposition? To induce short lifetimes for extraterrestrial civilizations from the simple fact that we have not found or been contacted by them seems a bit presumptuous. It assumes 1) that we have *not* as yet been contacted, either directly or indirectly (I contend that we have)*;* 2) that extraterrestrials would *want* to make full contact with us if they could (ETi's message implies that they don't); and 3) that our technology and effort in this regard has been in any way sufficient to the task, given the size of the Milky Way galaxy at 100,000 light-years across.

I do not think it follows that *intelligent* lifeforms tend like lemmings to extinct themselves for whatever reason. One could probably posit that some fraction of alien civilizations do, but to generalize this outcome for everyone out there, or even to a majority, seems wrong somehow. It seems to me that an *intelligent* species should, by definition, exhibit *at least* an ability to effect its own long-term survival, for heaven's sake. What's the point of being fully "intelligent" otherwise?

The winner of the 2006 Carl Sagan Medal, David Grinspoon, has argued that once a civilization develops, it might overcome all threats to its survival and thus last for an indefinite period of time, making the value for *L* potentially billions of years.

In 1961, Drake and his colleagues put the number of technological civilizations in our galaxy at up to 10, as we see in the figure below.

R^* = 10/year (10 stars formed per year, on the average over the life of the galaxy)

f_p = 0.5 (half of all stars formed will have planets)

n_e = 2 (stars with planets will have 2 planets capable of developing life)

f_l = 1 (50% of these planets will develop life)

f_i = 0.01 (1% of which will be intelligent life)

f_c = 0.01 (1% of which will be able to communicate)

L = 10,000 years (which will last 10,000 years) result:

N = 10 × 0.5 × 2 × 1 × 0.01 × 0.01 × 10,000 = **10**

Current estimates put the number of intelligent civilizations in our galaxy anywhere between 0 and 182 million, as shown below.

R^* = 7/year,

f_p = 0.4, n_e = 0,

f_l = 0.13,

f_i = 10^-9,

f_c = 0,

L = 304 years

result:

N = 7 × 0.4 × 0 × 0.13 × 10^-9 × 0 × 304 = **0**

$R* = 7/\text{year}, f_p = 1, n_e = 0.2\, f_l = 0.13, f_i = 1, f_c = 1,$ and $L = 10^9$ years result:

$N = 7 \times 1 \times 0.2 \times 0.13 \times 1 \times 1 \times 10^9 =$ **182 million**

Except for the value R* (the average rate of star formation per year in our galaxy), we really don't have any good idea what values to put in the other variables of the equation. Thus, we don't know if there are ten or a million intelligently inhabited planets in our galaxy. How can we? We're starting with almost zero data. The best anyone can really do is guess, which is never very satisfactory in science. If intelligent life has generated on ten or a million planets in our galaxy over the last two billion years, then one or more outposts of these civilizations could be maintaining stations a good deal less than a hundred light-years away from us. If the number is closer to ten, as Drake's equation predicts, then the chances are that their *home* planets are located well out of HRMS's search range. This doesn't mean, however, that they have not already surveyed, mapped, explored and colonized a substantial part of the galaxy by now.

Since curiosity and intelligence appear to be strongly correlated, this means that almost any intelligent race will make for the stars just as soon as it can, if for no other reason than to see what all is out there. We humans have been attempting something similar, though we haven't gotten very far, as yet. But then, we're quite new at the game, and winning in space isn't exactly easy.

Myths and apponents

There are many apponents to "Big Space," especially these days. It seems fashionable today to be against the development of space; such expensive, pie-in-the-sky endeavors appear to have little to do with the real world or the bottom line.

One reason for exploring and colonizing space is long-term survival, which trumps any pecuniary considerations of the bottom line. In biogalactic terms, survival for a species *depends* on its ability to expand its numbers in outer space, since once accomplished, it becomes much less likely that a species can be wiped out by either cosmic or self-inflicted causes. A species well colonized in space is relatively impervious to catastrophic cosmic or local changes, like solar hiccups, polar shifts, comet strikes, and so forth. On the other hand, planet-bound races have nowhere to go or hide. They might flee deep underground, for a while, but this will not stave off extinction for very long. The farther out a species extends itself, the safer it becomes, since even supernovas can then become survivable. A supernova is the explosion of a massive supergiant star, which can release as much energy as the total output of the sun during its 10 billion year lifetime. On average, a supernova occurs about once every 50 years in a galaxy the size of the Milky Way. Their radius of destruction can be many light-years. So the "bottom line" here is that planet-bound species are sitting ducks.

Some scientists argue that the distances between the stars are simply too immense to make space exploration feasible, for us or anybody else. Such beliefs do not really stand up to the numbers, however. Very simply, here's why:

The earth is 4.5 billion years old, our sun about 4.8 billion. Homo sapiens have existed on this planet (as such) for around 200,000 years. *Half* of the stars in the Milky Way galaxy, however, are estimated to be an average of 6.3 billion years old. That's 1.5 billion years older than our sun!

When we posit the existence of other intelligent species, we must be cognizant of the fact that some extraterrestrial civilizations will have been gathering knowledge, travelling in space, and expanding their purview of reality and the universe for *billions* of years. Since our galaxy has a diameter of 100,000 light-years, such an ETi could have traversed the entire Milky Way galaxy, from one end to the other, up to a few *thousand* times by now. To do this they would merely need to move objects, or themselves, through the vacuum of space at an average velocity of 10% of the speed of light. Ten percent can be considered a conservative estimate since even we humans, with our four-hundred-year-old science, could probably push the needle up to about 5% of the speed of light, should the idea ever more than just occur us.

So if an ETi civilization originating, let's say, one-thousand light-years from Earth began exploring or colonizing the galaxy 1.5 billion years ago, to reach Earth they would need to extend their sphere of influence at an average rate of one light-year every 150,000 years! Of course, this means that for every one light-year ETi travelled, they would be required to sit and consolidate on that planet or point in space for about 149,990 years before setting out on the *next* one light-year journey. That's a lot of down time. I don't think too many exploring sentients are going to be willing to sit put that long between jumps. So while the enormity of space is certainly one thing, *time* is quite another. This is to say, over very long stretches of time, many, many things become possible. *Very* possible.

Other anti-SETI arguments advanced over the years include those of Shklovskii, Dobzhansky and Mayer, who assert the fantastic unlikelihood of human intelligence being replicated. The argument falls apart, it seems to me, because it assumes that humanoid intelligence is the *only* kind of intelligence possible. Yes, the chances against a perfect replica of human beings evolving on another planet are immense beyond imagining, but this is as far as the argument is valid. That intelligence can take many forms is evident even on Earth inasmuch as many species exhibit different levels and types of intelligence or proto-intelligence. Human intelligence just happens to be the *dominant* one on Earth. The opportunistic and unpredictable nature of evolution means that many different permutations of intelligence are tried on every planet harboring life. Some will produce intelligence inferior to that of human beings while others should be expected to produce intelligence substantially superior.

Humancentric thinking is also expressed in what has been called Hart's paradox, that one cannot have *abundant* extraterrestrial life without abundant evidence for it on Earth. If the events we are about to discuss are any indication, such a self-impressed view becomes laughable. Shklovskii raises an interesting point, though, when he asserts that unlike conventional science, which begins with observations, SETI *searches* for observations. To be more precise about it, SETI searches for one very specific kind of observation -- radio-waves. In fact, NASA's eyes were willed shut to other forms data for reasons no more ingenious than that of scientific political correctness.

The hypothesis that different forms of non-humanoid intelligence may exist was discussed at the 1979 "Life in the Universe" conference. At this NASA-sponsored symposium, anthropologist Bernard Campbell pointed out that SETI searches are "tuned" to find signs of only *humanoid* intelligence. I'm not sure what phenotype has to do with intelligence, but the observation makes a good point in that it suggests that other kinds of intelligence may exist, kinds we have less than a clue about. What seems important is not so much the casement in which a brain resides but the brain, itself. What other *kinds* of brains, or intelligence, could we be talking about? The possibilities may be endless.

In 1987, Ames Researcher Center manager John Billingham said:

> "We know nothing about the other people out there. We don't know where to look. We don't know how long to look. We don't know what frequency to look on. We don't know whether to come back to the same source later on to look again. We don't know what polarization to look in. We don't know what sort of pattern of signal we're looking for. We don't know whether it has any modulation on it or not. When you get through with this list, it's no wonder people begin to balk.... Really, the bottom line is that we don't know what it takes to detect extraterrestrial intelligence."

Adding insult to this self-inflicted injury was the conclusion of Dartmouth psychologist John C. Baird:

"If advanced civilizations exist, but in a wildly alien form,   located in effect along very different physical, biological, and psychological dimensions, then all the observation time spent at the most sophisticated telescopes will be for naught. The aliens we seek will be going about their business in an alternate universe we are forever prohibited from learning anything about. Once this truth is realized, there will remain little point in continuing the search, since the target civilization will forever lie outside the scope of human comprehension."

This really is a pessimistic line to take. Such prolonged meditations must surely become a self-fulfilling prophecy. It seems to me that one form of intelligence really should be able to recognize and communicate with another form of intelligence. Scientific brainwashing need not override our innate abilities in this area; sometimes just using our eyes and brain will lead us to what we search for. Is a little more looking and listening and a little less science really asking too much?

The reason scientists have not detected the existence of extraterrestrials using the SETI paradigm may be as simple as *anthropic bias*. When applied to SETI, the principle would contend that if you collect a million radio-waves from space and none of them appear intelligently produced, then maybe the aliens don't communicate with or use radiowaves. An observer who looks *only* for intelligently produced radio-waves will either find them or not find them. If ETi were to use something *other* than radio-waves, then the ETI investigators would be quite out of luck.

As it happened, ETi did *not* use radio-waves to contact Earth (wouldn't you know). Let's now have a look at what *was* used, instead.

"If you look long enough into the void the void begins to look back through you." -- Friedrich Nietzche

Three
Here I am, H.B.

The playing fields were alive with the sound of cheering crowds up and down the northeastern corridor of America that October night ... the night ETi came to visit.

The first ETi signal arrived at a little before 8 p.m. on Friday evening, October 9, 1992, three days before HRMS was commenced. The Peekskill fireball was not just some inexplicable and pointless hovering or flying about, it had both a destination and a purpose. Its destination was a small town about twenty-seven miles north of New York City, as the crow flies. Its purpose was to communicate an immediate, or, actually, a preemptive, response to what NASA-Ames and NASA-JPL were about to start doing the following Monday.

Let's begin with the brief "Associated Press" article about this cosmic fireball. The item was printed in the New York "Daily News" on October 11th, 1992, the day before HRMS was commenced.

It's bird, plane ... meteor

A meteor showered skies over the East with glowing streaks of light Friday night, sprinkling debris near planes and prompting a deluge of telephone calls to authorities, officials said.

"It was just a big green ball of fire with a tail behind it," said John Law of Camden, W.Va.

The shooting lights were the Draconids, a display of meteors that passes through the Western Hemisphere every Oct. 9, said National Weather Service meteorologist Rich Mamrosh.

Ken Batty, a meteorologist in Charleston, W.Va., said, "Some pilots are reporting falling debris from up around 35,000 to 39,000 feet."

Sightings were also reported in Pennsylvania, New York, Maryland, Virginia, Washington D.C. and North Carolina. Peter Wolf, a meteorologist at Virginia's Richmond Airport, said, "The tower reported it looking like an aircraft burning up."

- The Associated Press

When I first heard about this meteor event on the television news on October 10th, my ET-meter was immediately pinged and very soon thereafter put on high alert. The floating of a highly conspicuous fireball seemed to me to be just the sort of reply we might receive while attempting to search for intelligent lifeforms. Since the idea of fireballs as augurs and "messengers from the gods" is very much a human thing, it occurred to me that an extraterrestrial that knew this about us could make very good use of this perennial human notion to issue a symbolic reply to NASA's alien hunting project.

Photo taken by Sarah Eichmiller of the Altoona Mirror from Mansion Park football stadium, using f/2.8 lens with 1/500s exposure on 3200 TMAX black & white film. Reprinted with permission from The Altoona Mirror.

The Peekskill fireball moved up the eastern United States like nobody's business, passing Washington D.C., Philadelphia and New York City. Due to the prime evening hour, the bright green bogey wowed thousands of night revellers from North Carolina and Kentucky to the shores of Lake Eerie. During the last twenty-three or so seconds of its 41-second atmospheric flight, more than fourteen different amateur video recordings were made of the shooting meteor in six states -- North Carolina, Ohio, Pennsylvania, West Virginia, Ohio and Virginia.

There couldn't have been a better time in America for a fireball to be seen and filmed. Friday nights in October are traditionally when hundreds of high school football games take place across the United States. Many spectators of these games bring video recorders with them and so have them at the ready. This distinctly American cultural proceeding accounted for most of the videos recorded that night.

The meteoroid hit our atmosphere at the near-grazing angle of 3.4 degrees, an *angle of incidence* considered highly unusual; 45 degrees is more typical. According to an article in "Nature" magazine, the meteor-fireball appeared to its first ground observers when it was flying over northern West Virginia, not far from the Green Bank Observatory, a facility about to participate in the HRMS project. From there it travelled in a northeasterly direction for about 420 miles before crashing to Earth.

When a meteoroid enters a planet's atmosphere at fifteen or twenty miles a second it begins to slow down. At this point, it is referred to as a meteor. This meteor was described by several eyewitnesses as being *lime-green* in color (what other color should a toe-dipping ETi have chosen?). One observer said it was brighter than the full moon, which was present in the sky that night. The "Washington Post" began it's October 10th article with the sentence: "A bright green light flashed across the region's skies about 8 p.m. last night, producing expressions of awe, wonder and perplexity." Except for one or two instances, the video recorders that filmed the event were unable to resolve this coloration due to their limited photo-response capabilities.

When the fireball was even with Washington D.C., it was at a height of approximately 25 miles. Here the fireball began to flicker at a frequency of 6 Hz and then split apart into seventy-odd fragments, as counted on two high-resolution still photographs made of the fireball.

A video recorded from the parking lot of a Burger King restaurant in Fairfax, Virginia shows the fireball already beginning to break up. The buildings that are visible on the ground provide a visceral sense of how fast the fireball was moving, and what it looked like in an urban setting. The words awesome and spectacular come to mind, but there is something else, something altogether spooky about something flying so fast and high in the night sky. Shooting stars have the same visual effect but these are generally pea-sized and so burn up quickly, offering only a brief viewing before they wink out. This bogey was a thousand times larger and therefore didn't completely burn up. Many of its large pieces just kept going and going.

At the end of the eight second recording, one man is heard asking, giddily, "What the hell was that?" Someone else with a voice remarkably similar to the actor, Tracey Walter, answers, "Beats the hell out of me." The verbal exchange makes me chuckle every time I hear it. (Like most of the other videos made that night, this video from Burger King can be viewed on the internet.)

Using what was an unprecedented surfeit of live amateur videos made of the fireball that night, a team of six scientists was able to publish an article in the prestigious science journal "Nature" entitled, "The orbit and atmospheric trajectory of the Peekskill meteorite from video records." Among other things, this densely scientific article traced the exact flightpath of the fireball, and provided a complete profile of its dynamical flight characteristics. These included a detailed time-resolved record of the object's fragmentation in the atmosphere, its speed at various points, its *radiant* (the point on the celestial sphere from which it originated), rate of decent, perihelion distance, inclination, orbital period, aphelion distance, longitude of ascending node, and more.

According to the article's authors, "never before has so much time-resolved dynamical detail ever been recorded for a fireball-meteorite event." They also stated, "These are the first motion pictures of a fireball from which a meteorite was recovered."

Another scientist who wrote a separate piece about the fireball for "Nature" magazine (its editor at the time) appeared in the same issue. He remarked: "It almost seems to have been trying to publicize its arrival, skimming low over a highly populated area of the United States before crashing to Earth..."

But then, as if the fireball were not nearly conspicuous enough, the fireball did something else even more amazing, though outrageous may be more like it, because a 27-pound fragment of the fireball then proceeded to crash through the "trunk" of a parked Chevrolet in Peekskill, New York. Actually, it wasn't so much the "trunk" of the car that was hit as it was the rear *signal-light* of a car -- the long and *narrow* signal-light of a car.

From beginning to end, the Peekskill meteor event was a scientist's dream. Everything that a measuring scientist could ever want to know about a meteor event was made available that night. Some things that a non-scientist like myself would like to know were also made available. A second "Daily News" article run on the 13th stated: "The (Peekskill) meteorite, measuring 11 inches by 4 inches by 5 inches... was studied by William Menke of the Lamont-Doherty Geological

Observatory in Palisades." Now, the dimensions of a 1980 Chevrolet Malibu's rear signal-lights are roughly 4-1/2 inches by 22 inches!

1980 Chevrolet Malibu owned by Michelle Knapp of Peekskill, New York. While watching TV at 7:50 p.m. she heard what sounded like a car crash outside her home. She investigated only to find a smoking meteorite underneath the trunk of her car. Reprinted with permission from "The Journal" (a Gannett newspaper).

Well, this certainly didn't leave much room for error. I mean, how *does* a 4 x 5 x 11-inch wide meteorite pluck out a 4-1/2-inch wide signal-light without also doing serious damage to either the chrome bumper beneath the signal-light *or* the slim chrome accent immediately above it? Notice how pristine the bumper looks. Look at the right and then the left signal-lights. The right one is completely gone, from one side to the other. Blind nature just doesn't do this sort of thing. Well, it *could* do it, but the notion seems a bit questionable. In any case, a question *was* set up by this meteor impact: was this the result of blind nature *or* intelligent action? It simply had to be one or the other.

Somewhere in the culturally programmed regions of my unconscious mind a voice was whispering that a meteor has to hit somewhere, that if such a thing *could* happen by chance, then it did happen by chance. The only problem was I wasn't listening. Yes, such a thing could happen by accident, but what if it didn't?

What if this was exactly what it looked like it was -- one awfully fine shot?

There was another freeky bulls-eye to consider here, though -- the town in which the impact happened. The town was important because both the name of the meteorite and of the event as a whole would bear that town's name. The final destination of the fireball was the New York town of *Peekskill!*

Of all possible names for *this* meteor event to take, Peekskill seemed amazingly apropos. It was as if to say, "Here's a small peek at *our* skill, baby." And, of course, there it was on the back end of a Chevy for all the world to see.

Over the next few days, the impacted car was shown on several television news broadcasts. The scene shown was that of a suburban driveway in Peekskill, New York, where the 27 pound meteorite had been recovered. The TV cameras seemed pinned to the backside of the overused Chevrolet, showing this gaping hole where its right rear *signal*-light used to be.

The item became something of a media sensation, which at the time was really saying something. The great American Quincentennial (Oct. 12, 1992) was right around the corner, after all. The media had been hyping that momentous occasion for weeks. Over one hundred tall ships from around the world were converging on New York Harbor even as I watched the Peekskill coverage. New York City was celebrating the quincentennial with a spectacular, once-in-a-lifetime procession of tall ships up the Hudson river. There would be parades everywhere, Grucci fireworks, the works. In South America, where the festivities, if anything, were even more lavish, Pope John Paul II was making a special trip to Santo Domingo to commemorate the occasion.

More than 100 tall ships—many of them famous antiques – from around the world converged on New York City's Hudson River to celebrate the American Quincentennial (500th anniversary of America's discovery).

Still, the fireball and its aftermath managed to steal air time. One TV network even used the "cosmic fender-bender" story as a commercial teaser for its evening news broadcast. One reason for this, though it was never mentioned, had to do with the clearly visible fact that the meteor had struck the *right* signal-light of the car, not the left. Indeed, there was something emphasized, even articulate, about this, something very true. It seemed to say, "*Right*, Ames! You bet we exist." This, anyway, was the first meaningful phrase to enter my mind upon viewing the meteor impact on my television screen. This meaning seemed reinforced by the fact that NASA-*Ames* was very soon to commence a *Targeted* Search for ETI.

The articulating nature of all this had been made possible by the precision of the impact. The words right, signal (-light), Ames, targeted, and Peekskill all added up to skill, not cosmic luck.

How long does an eagle need to grasp the totality of a landscape? Does its eye see all or does it concentrate only on that for which it searches? The less powerful human eye does not generally ascertain a scene in its entirety, but at that moment, sitting before my television, one nervous wrist dislodging an October fly, I knew that I was looking at mankind's first communication from the stars. It was then that I realized that something intelligible was going to be written, as it were, on the car's license plate. After all, only an inch or two separates the license plate from either of the car's signal-lights, and what better reason could there be for selecting a particular car in Peekskill if not to draw attention to what effectively could be written there? In fact, if something salient and meaningful *wasn't* to be found there, I figured my theory of ET causation would be in serious trouble.

By now the seconds were ticking away fast. The on-site reporter was covering the story exactly the way one would expect a mainstream TV reporter to cover something like this -- lots of trivia and tongue-in-cheek banter. Quickly, then, I took in and memorized the license plate: it read: *4GF-933*.

For one obvious reason my attention was immediately pulled to the numbers appearing on the right portion of the license plate, to the numbers **933**. The first thing I picked up about these numbers was their symmetry: $3 \times 3 = 9$, or $3^2 = 9$. It was a tidy relationship, but what, if anything, did *this* mean? I knew the numbers had to mean something, otherwise my fondest suspicions would fall apart. Then it hit me. The date the impact event occurred, October *9,* was *3* days before the 12th. And, yes, *two* historically momentous things were going down on the 12th, not just one: America's "Big 5-0-0", commemorating the day in 1492 Christopher Columbus discovered America, and the activation of NASA's massive hunt for extraterrestrials, HRMS. *Of course!*

The aimers of the Peekskill fireball were clearly drawing attention to these two human milestone events, and why not! Then I realized the significance of my first observation about the numbers 933 concerning their mathematical relationship.

HRMS (3) X Quincentennial (3) = or *yields* Peekskill event (9)

It was as if to say, when these two *particular* historic milestones are paired together, the result yields more than the sum of their parts. That is, 3 x 3 equals significantly more than 3 + 3.

Of course, the TV media wasn't mentioning any of this. I couldn't imagine why they weren't, but that's the media for you. Mention was made of the newsworthy fact, for example, that the car's owner did not own any meteorite insurance, but there was not a word about signal-lights, or towns with apropos-sounding names, nothing about the curiously pregnant timing of the thing, not even in jest. No matter, I figured the media would get around to it eventually, for it was all very plain to me.

The "Gannett Suburban Newspaper" published an article on the 13th called "Meteorite's landing spot a star attraction." One sentence read:

"Yesterday afternoon, Knapp -- who was celebrating her 18th birthday -- sat on the steps leading to her white-and-green house as about a half-dozen people gawked at her damaged car and the small crater beneath it."

Hello!

In addition to being America's 500th birthday, and the date of HRMS activation, October 12th was also Miss Knapp's 18th birthday! It was her coming of age, as it were. Michelle Knapp was the young woman whose car was perforated by the Peekskill meteorite. It was a lovely coincidence, but for me it was a coincidence that broke the back of all of the other "coincidences" adorning this meteor event. Although the chances of this were only 1 in 365, it might as well have been one in a million.

Miss Knapp later sold her twelve-year-old, now all but useless Chevy to a collector for $25,000. She reportedly sold her 27-pound "Peekskill meteorite" for an additional $50,000. Nice birthday present.

The Peekskill event certainly *looked* like it had been intelligently crafted. It had all the earmarks -- uncanny aim, uncanny salience, perfect timing. Moreover, extraterrestrials just happened to be the thing we were *looking* for at the time, by George!

But the very idea -- its crazy

Is it? Let's take a moment to address this. The objection might be rephrased like this: how could *anyone*, advanced aliens included, hit a Chevrolet tail-light with a rock from space? The question is a fair one.

Glib answer? ETi does not need to be fair, nor are they just anyone. If ETi did this, then obviously they possess substantially superior knowledge, skill and know-how than we do. The probable fact of the matter is that the ETi responsible for Peekskill is *millions* of years more advanced than us, not just hundreds or thousands. This could easily account for what happened here.

Next on the objection list would be *why?* Why would extraterrestrials do something so off topic and trivial as uncork a car's rear signal-light when it would be so much clearer and simpler to just dispatch a communication via radio-waves, as expected? Why the artifice?

Here are the probable answers. First, ETi was not interested in communicating with us in a way that would force them to completely reveal themselves to us. A formal and direct communication would have caused massive interference in our world; it would change everything, actually for *both* parties, overnight. It would have been too much too fast. Under the circumstances, it made much more sense to dip a toe in human waters before taking the plunge (if plunging is on the agenda).

Consider the upshot if full and unmistakable contact *had* been made? Militaries all over the world would be brought to high alert. Whole populations might panic and lose sleep. The press and media would immediately launch into "24/7" mode with wild and gloomy speculation. Religious leaders and soothsayers would pawn impending doom from the "evil" aliens. Corporations would angle for deals. Intelligence agencies would scheme and throw every dirty trick in the book toward the mission of penetrating and stealing whatever high-tech secrets they could lay their hands on. Then there would be the thousand-and-one questions from scientists. Oh, good lord, no!

Making contact with another world is not the kind of thing one rushes headlong and precipitously into. It makes great sense to test the waters first. Who knows, the water might be ice cold. What's more, there will be protocols, protocols possibly born of long experience. For all we know they may have already determined humankind to be unsuitable for full and direct contact. I mean, *just look at us!* Three or four "peace wars" going on at any one time, corruption at the highest levels, off-the-chart greed, mass starvation, cruelty so ponderous as to stagger the imagination and darken the mind. No, it is hard to imagine that it could make any sense for advanced and civilized alien beings to intermingle with or have very much to do with such creatures.

If what I had readily inferred from this event up to this point was the sum total of my observations, I don't think it would have made much difference to me. I was already convinced at this point that the Peekskill event could not have been a random act of nature. The odds were simply too outrageous, the words and meanings too apropos and right on for it all to be an accident. Perhaps if all of this had happened at some other time, I wouldn't have thought very much of any of it; but on that particular SETI's eve, I was incapable of ascribing these proceedings to anything or anyone else but an extraterrestrial intelligence.

What I didn't know at the time, however, was that the articulating details mentioned above represented but the tip of a large iceberg, an iceberg composed of many, many other astounding details and lines of inference. I also knew nothing as yet about two other unprecedented and curiously eloquent impact events, one of which had already happened.

"Do you want to know who you are? Don't ask. Act! Action will delineate and define you." -- Thomas Jefferson

Four
Chris Columbus?

In one crucial respect NASA's experimental "search" for alien life was different from any other scientific endeavor ever conducted. It's object of study involved subjects who had every potential to be substantially superior in every important way to the humans conducting the experiment. This extant contingency had the potential, therefore, to render NASA's investigation not only useless, but, much more, to switch around the roles of experimenter and subject.

Every psychologist knows that in the great bulk of experimental situations involving sentient humans, a subject who is aware that he/she is being experimented upon or studied will behave differently from one who is not aware of this. That the scientists conducting the experimental probe (HRMS) could end up being the subjects of their own experiment never occurred to them, not even after I pointed the possibility out to them, or maybe *because* I pointed it out to them.

However clever and upbeat a commencement of HRMS on the Quincentennial Columbus Day might have seemed to its progenitors, the publicity stunt turned out to be rather boneheaded for a number of reasons. If a child were to appear before the Joint Chiefs of Staff and demand all their latest weapons to play with, it might have come close to ETi's double-take at the idea of being systematically searched for and "surveyed" by *this* federal agency from the planet Earth. Whether the affront was taken with a grain of salt, with annoyance, or even outrage seems a matter open to discussion, though I hardly think one should be too sanguine about this uncertainty.

But NASA's symbolic pairing could only be considered *totally* boneheaded if NASA refused to acknowledge ETi's symbolic rejoinder, because if NASA did decide to receive it, then its chosen symbolism would be tantamount to a SETI success!

But it was not to be. Scientists love their rules more than anything else in the universe, and are not too swift when it comes to things, or entities, lying well outside their beloved box. For the SETI investigators there could be no consideration made for an extraterrestrial's point of view or way of doing things. It was either extraterrestrial radiowaves or nothing, even though the possibility existed that an extrasolar world might take a very dim view of a species with a history like ours poking around. Some hyper-paranoid worlds, for whom the past is never past, might even feel it their solemn duty to take concrete steps to put a check on NASA's unsanctioned snooping.

Christopher Columbus discovers America (Oct. 12, 1492)

John Vanderlyn's painting, Landing of Columbus, commissioned in 1836/1837,
depicts Christopher Columbus' landing in the West Indies in 1492. Columbus
holds the royal banner of Spain, laying claim to the land. He holds a sword in
his right hand and his hat lies at his feet. Behind him are the other men who
traveled on the voyage, including the captains of the Niña and the Pinta, who
carry the banner of King Ferdinand and Queen Isabella. Some of the men
kneel on the ground, apparently looking for gold. Ships are visible in the water
in the background. To the right, natives of the island — which they called
Guanahani and Columbus named San Salvador — look on from the woods.

Was the tacit threat of invasion and genocide *inherent* in NASA's chosen symbolism to be taken seriously, or was it just a blundering P.R. stunt to garner attention from its own teeming masses? It seems inquiring minds wanted to know -- *for sure.* Or maybe it was just a really good time for a fresh *reading* to be made. So who *are* we with the very poor manners?

Fortunately, an ethically principled ETi agency appears to have taken up the fact-finding mission. This was accomplished by setting up an experimental situation on and completely around our world (as we'll see later) in which both an overture was floated and one or more hypotheses were queried.

One thing ETi's signal tested was whether or not humans, or scientists, possess a historical *conscience.* Interesting word conscience; it has two syllables -- con and science. If NASA, or anyone else picked up on their meteoritic *symbol* and thus its intelligent nature, then this might support the hypothesis that humans do possess a conscience. It might even suggest that we rather suddenly became aware of the *faux pas* released on a sentient galaxy, and will endeavor not to repeat such in the future. If, on the other hand, neither NASA nor anyone else picked up their perfectly tendered signals, then this would indicate a complete lack of historical or moral conscience, and thus bring our motives for the SETI probe into question.

For the experiment to work their meteoritic *stimulus* would need to be couched in a suitably unscientific and inconclusive fashion. Anything much more conclusive would have run the risk of spoiling the experiment, not to mention the entire embargo put in place who knows how long ago. This meant literally stuffing the stimulus event with improbable but saliently articulate coincidences, details that would not necessarily attain that scientific critical mass of acceptability. Therein would lie the test.

Before we take a small microscope to the Peekskill meteor event in Chapter 5, and those other events that followed or preceded it, it should be helpful and informative to review the accomplishments and legacy of Christopher Columbus in the New World. Maybe by doing this we can see what all the fuss was about. Who was this man who changed world as we know it with his voyages of discovery?

C. Columbus

Portrait of Christopher Columbus, explorer & navigator; discoverer of the "New World" October 12, 1492.

Christopher Columbus was an iconic adventurer who looked for opportunity wherever and whenever he could find it. To be fair to him, Columbus exhibited some very positive aspects in his younger days -- before power, fame and wealth changed him. He was kind, principled, and ambitious in a positive and knowledge seeking way. In many respects he was a man of his times, a product of his age. Although he made many mistakes and enemies, his bold gamble paid off and he changed both history and the maps of the world.

As part of the terms for undertaking his dangerous westward voyage, Columbus was granted ten percent of any profits made from his voyages. In addition, he eventually received the noble ranks of Viceroy and Admiral from the Spanish Crown. His Royal commission gave him the use of three ships. The Santa Maria, his flagship, was classified as a carrack, and was a four masted ocean-going sailing ship. The Niña and Pinta were three-masted carousels.

After a long lay-over in the Canary Islands for repairs, the three ships departed West on September 6, 1492. Now, Columbus did not sally forth into the unknown for reasons of science or religious altruism; he went, as his own diaries and letters state, to encounter and seize wealth belonging to others. He would seize this wealth by whatever means necessary in order to enrich both himself and his sponsors.

On the morning of October 12, 1492, land was sighted by a crew member named Rodrigo de Triana. There was some dispute over who actually spotted it first. The king and queen had offered a reward for the first man to see land, and so Columbus claimed the reward based on the fact that he had seen lights on the night of the 11th and pointed them out to some crew members. It is not known with any certainty which island in the Bahamas was found but it may have been Watling's Island.

Columbus and his crews rejoiced at finding what they thought was an island in the Far East. His chief mission had been to find a trade route to the orient. Much was made of the natives they found. They were described as naked, friendly, impressionable, poor, and quick to learn. At his first meeting with the island natives on the 13th, Columbus made it plain that he was interested in finding gold. He noticed that some of the natives wore gold rings in their noses. He was told about a king to the south that had large quantities of the ore, but he never found either the king or his gold. Perhaps the natives were anxious to see Columbus and his men sail somewhere else or where certain of their enemies lived.

The yearning for gold drove Columbus from one island to another. On October 28th he reached Cuba, which he believed to be Cipango (Japan), because he came to a river that his ships could easily sail into, unlike many of the other islands he had seen. He was not greeted in a friendly manner. Maybe this was the realm of the king of whom he had been told.

Columbus discovered many major islands during his three voyages including Puerto Rico, Cuba, Jamaica and the Bahamas. His main base of operations was Hispañola (modern day Haiti and Dominican Republic). On returning there on the 22nd of November, he found the small fort he had established at La Navidad destroyed and everyone killed, which must have been a shock to him. After this he was determined that the natives should know the power and justice of Spain.

In 1493 Columbus returned with an invasion force of seventeen ships and with the titles of viceroy and governor of the Caribbean islands and mainland, a position he held until 1500. When it became clear that gold would not be found in the quantities he had hoped, he promptly instituted policies of slavery (encomiendo) and systematic extermination of the native Taino population. As a result, Taino populations were reduced from perhaps eight million to about three million by 1496, and by 1500 to around 100,000. His policies remained in place until well after his final departure from the New World, with the result that by 1514 the Spanish census of the island showed barely 22,000 indians remaining alive. By 1542, only 200 were recorded and sometime afterward the Tainos became extinct.

In the summer of 1494, Columbus sent a request to the King and Queen in Spain for permission to enslave the population. The sovereieigns refused his request, but Columbus, desperate for cash, exported over 500 Taino slaves anyway, with about 200 of them dying on the voyage. Queen Isabella ordered the remaining slaves returned to their homes and freed.

The proportion of indigenous Caribbean natives killed by the Spanish in a single generation was greater than eighty percent. The atrocities visited upon their populations by the European invaders were legion, with perhaps as many as one hundred million, or well over 90 percent, being either killed or infected with european germs for which they had no immunological defense.

Historical accounts by Las Casas and others are fairly replete with atrocities such as mass hangings and roastings. Children were hacked into pieces and used as dog feed. The Spaniards made bets as to who could slit a man in two, or cut off his head at one blow. They tore babies from their mothers by their feet and dashed their heads against the rocks, or spitted their bodies together on their swords.

If this treatment was meant to instill in the natives "a proper respect" for the European God, the Indians will have surely scoffed at the grandiose notion, for the indians saw they were being systematically despoiled of their kingdoms, dignity, homes, liberties and lives.

Following closely upon Columbus's heels were the Conquistadors, Spanish armies comprised largely of misfits, criminals and opportunists. Theirs is another story, but it is a story every bit as horrific for mainland populations as Columbus's was for the Caribbeans, if not more so.

Time for time

None of this was considered very important to the progenitors of HRMS. Science considers itself to be above such soft academic terrains. Scientists like to stick to what's real, with what is or can be known with statistical certainty. As such they stay close to the hypothesis and experiment at hand, not go wandering off into historical reveries and conjecture.

If time is the great absolver of past crimes, then NASA could be excused for overlooking this largely Columbian legacy. But what is time to a star traveller? Five hundred years might be considered as nothing to beings that may have more or less transcended mortality. Five hundred years is a long time on a stationary planet, but for sentients able to push the needle up past 50 percent or more of the speed of light, or able to make use of some exotic quirk of physics, such time frames might be considered quite short. If so, then what happened in and to the "New World" must have been just awful to watch.

As much as I could go on and on about the Spanish Conquistadors, and the treatment of the North American Indians by the northern European settlers, this begins to stray beyond the scope of Columbus and this book. Besides, I could run the risk of numbing the reader with holocaust overload, and we wouldn't want that. Instead, I'll just close this chapter by suggesting that science works well in most experimental circumstances involving physical phenomena, often exceedingly well, but it works not so well -- or not at all -- when making inquiry into intelligent beings. Human non-receptivity to the events of 1992-4 clearly attest to this.

Science with its small collection of ETi-investigating techniques was not up to the task for which it was given. This seems the simple history of it.

Play not with paradoxes. That caustic which you handle in order to scorch others may happen to sear your own fingers and make them dead to the quality of things. - George Eliot

Five
The quest for ETi

Chapter three cited my initial observations about the Peekskill meteorfall, particularly its quite peculiar impact of a parked Chevrolet in Peekskill, New York. Although the story received substantial topical coverage on the10th and 11th of October, the incident was no longer "news" by the 13th. Could it be that this untold story had been laid squarely and exclusively in my lap? Needless to say, I immediately went with it. In fact, I became rather obsessed with learning everything I could about the event, about the science of meteors and comets, and many other things relating to the subject. By the end of October, 1992, I was fully engaged in my own SETi project, half expecting the government or some other individual to beat me to the oracular punch. No one ever did.

During the course of my research I learned many interesting things to support my thesis of ETi intervention. Every day seemed to bring some new revelation, some new angle or twist to what I could only assume was an extraterrestrial communication or warning of some kind. What I always found was the same ridiculous precision, but it was never precision for mere precision's sake; there was always a clear and precise meaning to be inferred. Here's an example. The article in "Nature" magazine revealed the recovered meteorite's weight in the very first sentence:

"...a 12.4-kg ordinary chondrite was recovered in Peekskill,
New York." ("Nature" - Vol. 367 - 17 February 1994)

12.4 kilograms works out to exactly 27.3373 pounds. This is because
1 kilogram equals 2.2 pounds. If we round off the number 27.3373,
we get 27.3. Call me superstitious but 27.3 looks an awful lot like
93.3 -- the numbers on the right side of the license plate!

93.3 .... 27.3

If this was intentional, then it was *quite* a trick. The meaning of
this mathematical allusion, taking into account the position of the
decimal points, will become clear a little later in this chapter.

Although no physical laws appeared to be broken, I never seriously
considered the Peekskill event an accident of nature. So long as the
possibility existed that the impact *wasn't* a blind accident of nature,
there was every reason to continue the quest, which meant according
the presumed interlocutor the benefit of a doubt. I was not only
willing but quite keen to do this.

Considering the various odds that were published for a meteor
hitting a particular car -- "a billion to one" and "several billions
to one" -- the odds of a meteor hitting a particular car's right or
left *tail-light* must therefore have been several tens or hundreds of
billions to one (*against* this happening). The margin for error here
was basically nil, yet as far as the media was ever concerned, the
meteor had merely struck "a car" or the "trunk of a car." Not once
was it mentioned that the object pulverized from one end to the
other was the right *tail-light* of a car. I never understood why this
perfectly obvious fact was never raised.

Peekskill meteorite - Swiss Meteorite Lab

So how *does* a five inch-wide rock from space navigate through a 5-inch wide car tail-light without ripping to shreds *either* the bumper beneath the tail-light *or* the thin chrome accent above it? Even more tantalizing than this was the question: how did the slim chrome accent just happen to *overscore* or crop the numbers "933" on that license plate? "Very carefully", sure, but this was over the top!

The "Gannett Suburban Newspaper" (now "The Journal") ran three separate stories about the impact side of the story. The first was circulated October 11th, followed by one on the 12th, and the third on the 13th. Three different reporters had their crack at the cosmic fenderbender. From the first article we learn that the meteorite's next stop was the American Museum of Natural History, where it would be studied and classified an H6 chondrite. A quote was taken in this article from Dr. William Menke of the Lamont-Doherty Geological Observatory, one of the first geologists at the scene: "It may turn out scientifically that this is a real breakthrough or an interesting thing that gets written on a list with 4,999 other meteorites."

From the second article we learn how Michelle Knapp, the original owner of the Chevrolet and meteorite, discovered the meteorite buried and still smoking beneath her car's trunk after hearing what sounded like a car crash outside. From this piece I also learned the name of Dr. Menke's associate, Dr. Mark Anders, a specialist in large impact craters. I would pick his brains on several occasions by telephone for information on the impact, as we'll see shortly.

The third *Gannett* story talked about crowds of up to 400 people gathering around the Knapp house near where the impact took place. It mentions the bidding to buy the meteorite from its lucky owner, and that three television news crews had been to the house. It also mentioned the fact that Monday, October 12, 1992 was that lucky owner's 18th birthday. That last one was the kicker for me.

I tried to contact Miss Knapp ("Mickey") on several occasions with the idea of interviewing her, but I was never able to. For whatever reason she did not seem very interested in being cornered for an interview, so I took the hint and stopped pursuing her.

All souls do what's true

We'll recall that the license plate numbers appearing on the right half of Michelle Knapp's license plate, "933", seemed to refer to the Peekskill event's timing with respect to the Big 5-0-0 and NASA's commencement of HRMS. At various times during the course of my investigation, I inferred other meanings from these curiously over-scored numbers, each interpretation as clear and necessary as the others (I'll cover about seven of them by the end of the book). Here is one of them.

All astronomers, and many others as well, know that the Earth revolves around the sun at an average distance of 93 million miles. Astronomers call it the Astronomical Unit, abbreviated A.U. They consider this number important enough that they use it to measure space. Earth lies 1 A.U. (93 million miles) from the sun. By comparison, our nearest star, Alpha Centauri Proxima, lies 4.3 A.U. from Earth. From this it occurred to me that **93** might easily represent our planet's Astronomical Unit. If this were the case, then the second **3** in **933** would then obviously refer to Earth, the *third planet* from the sun. How apropos and complete, I thought. In 93/3, therefore, we had a remarkably salient and descriptive handle for Earth. It was as if to say, "Come in 933, this is XYZ calling (anybody home?)."

It isn't at all hard to imagine an alien civilization using this form of moniker to succinctly identify and refer to its neighbors. A planet's A.U. is an extremely important piece of information; it governs whether or not life will or can appear on it. Computer simulations indicate that if the Earth's orbit were only five per cent smaller than it actually is, there would have been a "runaway greenhouse" effect causing ambient temperatures to boil off the oceans in their entirety. Conversely, if the average distance between the Earth and Sol were as little as one or two per cent larger, the world's mean temperature would have plunged to minus fifty degrees fahrenheit billions of years ago, causing permanent glaciation.

Although not apparently emphasized by the ETi aimer(s), the alpha-numeric figures on the *left* side of the license plate, **4GF**, were not exactly devoid of salient meaning, either. The radio-astronomers at Ames Research Center and JPL were about to start scanning *only* "G" and "F" type stars in the hope of finding intelligent microwave signals emanating from them. Astronomers consider G and F spectral type stars the only kinds of stars around which life-bearing planets could possibly exist. Some 512 stars of spectral type "G" are currently believed to be located within 100 light-years of Earth, the farthest distance in space studied by The Targeted Search. Another 300 or so stars of spectral type "F" are believed to be located within the same distance.

Here's the titillating question: does this mean to say there are *four* intelligently inhabited G and F type stars known to Peekskill's dispatcher? Or would this refer to the existence of four life-bearing planets within the NASA's search range, planets with more simple forms of life living on them? These and other variations of the question can only intrigue, and until a *two*-sided exchange can be arranged, the question will have to go unanswered. But it definitely seems a number to store away someplace.

Augur things

As noted earlier, there is a perennial human belief that fireballs are intelligent signs, or warnings, from beyond. Indeed, for many centuries, fireball and comets have been thought to portend things, usually very large or catastrophic things, like the death of a king, a great flood, pestilence, the destruction of an empire, and the like. As it happens, a fireball provided ETi with an extremely serviceable *stylus* with which to send a communication to our world.

Famously, Montezuma, the ruler of the Aztecs in Columbus's time, saw a comet in the sky and from this predicted the imminent doom of his empire. The prediction was uncannily prescient because in a few short years his enormous empire would be in a complete shambles. One can almost wonder if that particular comet was also sent by the same intelligence to warn Montezuma of the carnage to come.

If we follow this line of reasoning to its logical *auguring* conclusion, then 933 should refer to a particular month and year, or in this case to March 1993 (93/3).

As observed earlier, this is just the sort of thing an entity familiar with its subject world would know and utilize in some useful way. By the time this particular reading of the numbers occurred to me in November, the time referenced was only 4-1/2 months away!

Okay, I thought, something extremely big was going down in March 1993 or 93/3. I distinctly remember wondering what it would possibly end up being. Whatever it was, I knew it was coming, and I knew it would be big, because there was no way the designers of this communique would overlook this. In fact, if something big *didn't* happen in 93/3, then there was something seriously wrong with my thinking, my whole theory.

Did something really big happen in March of 1993? Of course it did. In fact, it turned out to be about the most spectacular thing to happen in our solar system in a hundred thousand years, or maybe a few million. This event is the subject of the next chapter. It was the *second* signal dispatched by the aimer.

A step back

When we look at the landscape or stage on which the first signalling event made itself known, we notice some significant facts. The most obvious of these may be the event's freakish and unprecedented essence. Sure, meteors fall to Earth all the time but never before had a meteoritic fireball ever been both filmed in the air *and* recovered on the ground.

Another rather glaring fact is that the Peekskill meteor garnered more public and media attention than any previous meteor event ever had. It was seen first-hand by thousands of night revelers up and down the eastern United States. It was photographed and filmed by more than two dozen night revellers from North Carolina and Kentucky to New York and Ohio. Millions of people all over the world probably read about it in their local newspapers. Just about every film documentary on the subject of meteors, comets or asteroids made subsequent to October 9, 1992 mentions it. Peekskill has become a kind of benchmark event in the meteoritic field.

One *could* find it a little strange that with so much attention given this event, so little was actually made of it. Not a word was to be found anywhere on its possible intelligent causation other than in your author's published and unpublished writings. The "discovery" did not give its discoverer the slightest notariety or mention. No magazine other than "MUFON Journal" and "UFO Universe" (defunct) would touch my story. I actually declined the latter offer to publish my story. Its editor was an old friend of mine from as early as my Carmine Street teenager days. Somehow releasing the news in this way didn't seem like the right thing to do. I didn't think his UFO readers wouldn't appreciate it, anyway. I knew by this time the general ho-hum attitude of the UFO community concerning my findings. I would be just one more pilgrim who *thought* he saw a UFO. Of course, Peekskill had nothing whatever to do with UFOs, but this wouldn't matter.

For its part, the MUFON Journal (Mutual UFO Network) accepted my article but the editor, Walt Andrus, demanded that I extirpate any direct reference to extraterrestrials from my article. This struck me as goofy and outrageous. Something about the Journal's strict scientific policy was the reason given. Sure, right! – a journal whose middle name is UFO not interested in an extraterrestrial communication. Give me a break! It is the kind of thing one can expect in this dizzy field, though, and makes about as much sense as NASA's alien-hunting policy of leaving all stones unturned in *its* quest for ETi.

The article entitled "Of fireballs good and old" (what a lousy title it seems now) was published in the May 1996 (Vol. 337) issue of MUFON UFO Journal. In the article I was allowed to wax deliriously on such things as the fact that physicists were able by the following year (1993) to reconstruct for only the fourth time in history both the original orbit in space and exact groundpath of a meteor after its fall; and, that the fireball's groundpath was determined by triangulation analysis, which was made possible by a frame by frame analysis of four of the fourteen recordings studied. These included the ones made in Fairfax, Virginia (38° 51' N, 77° 19' W); Johnstown, Pennsylvania (40° 20' N, 78° 56' W); Pittsburgh, Pennsylvania (40° 26' N, 80° 01' W); and Willoughby, Ohio (41° 38' N, 81° 26' W).

Quoting from my article now -- "A frame rate of 30 frames per second (60 video fields per second) was assumed by the analyzing team, which consisted of four Canadians, one Czech, and one American. Their analysis revealed a pre-atmospheric velocity for the fireball of more than 15 km per second. According to their report to the British journal Nature, "The duration of the event (10-20 times longer than typical fireballs), the use of data from four widely spaced stations, the large number of points (254), and the excellent (1/60 s) time resolution all contributed to a rather precise preatmospheric velocity and apparent radiant.""

The piece went on and on about technical stuff, but what did any of this mean? These details were not important in themselves. What was important was what a good many of them *meant*.

I never went back to the peevish and contradictory world of UFOs after this. Well, there was a 55-minute lecture I gave to the 12th (or was it the 13th?) Annual UFO Congress in August of 2002, but I was barely able to cover the first three chapters in this book in the piddling time allotted me. Nor did it help very much that my slides were all upside down.

There were many other things about Peekskill to snag an observer's attention. Whatever stone I turned over, the result was almost always the same -- *snake-eyes*. Eventually, the pair of pips on each die began very much to resemble a pair of eyes -- sagacious, quipster eyes.

Here's one good example. Because of the meteorfall's prime time evening hour (8 p.m.), resulting in a large number of videos being made available for study, scientists were able by a process known as triangulation analysis to determine an exact flight path for the fireball. Please take a moment to study the map provided.

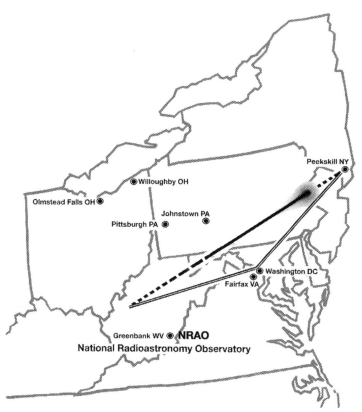

Map shows flight path of the Peekskill fireball (Oct. 9, 1992, 7:49 p.m.).
Long dashed line plus solid line (~700 km) represents the visible portion
of the meteor's descent; the short dashed line is the theoretical initial
(undocumented) portion of the flight path. Green Bank, WV is the site
of the National Radio and Astronomy Observatory (NRAO), a major
participant in the HRMS (SETI) project, and the birthplace of SETI.
Towns mentioned are some of the locations where video recordings of the
fireball were made.

The main article in "Nature" magazine began with the sentence:
"On 9 October 1992, a bright fireball appeared over West Virginia,
travelled some 700 km in a northeasterly direction..." Not mentioned
in any publication or film that I was able to lay a hand on, however,
was the clearly observable fact that Washington D.C. just happened
to have the best seat in the house from which to watch the lime-green
bogey streak by. When we connect the dots between the fireball's first

observed location in West Virginia "700 kilometers" out, its endpoint in Peekskill, and Washington D.C., we observe that a nearly perfect isosceles triangle (an triangle with two equal sides) is formed. Well, HRMS was a *federal* project, wasn't it? What other burg should have gotten so long and good a look at the fireball as it broke apart into fragments? Pittsburgh?

The press and media also failed to notice that the National Radio and Astronomy Observatory (NRAO), the West Virginia birthplace of SETI, happens to be located on a kind of parallel with the first *eyeball* observations made of the fireball. As mentioned earlier, NRAO was one of several observatories that participated in the HRMS project. Why, the fireball might have waved at the SETI investigators who were probably calibrating their instuments that night.

Not mentioned anywhere either was the meteor's *angle of impact*. Dr. Mark Anders of the Lamont-Doherty Geological Observatory told me in a phone interview that he had ascertained that the meteor went through the car at an angle of 77 degrees. Of course, it would *have* to be "77" degrees. What salient sense would any other impact angle have made? In the *human* vernacular, this number connotes luck, of course, which is the *opposite* of skill. No question about it, the concept of "luck vs. skill" is at the heart of the whole mystery. So which was it, luck or skill? Hmmm, let's see now .... *ah, go on!*

One *sporadic* for the road

Perhaps the most important single message delivered that October night derived from the fact that the meteor was *not* a draconid meteor, although everyone, including Dr. Mencke initially thought it was. This was quite understandable because on October 9, 1992, the Draconid meteor shower just happened to be at its peak. The newspapers all reported as much. But, as just stated, the meteor-fireball was *not* a Draconid meteor; it was what's known as a *sporadic* meteor, instead.

Sporadics, as they are called, refer to meteors that are not associated with a meteor shower.

This information came to me from Dr. Martin Prinz, curator of meteorites at the American Museum of Natural History in New York City. According to Dr. Prinz, the Peekskill meteor could *not* have been a Draconid for the simple reason that it arrived from the South, not from the North as all Draconids do.

The northern circumpolar constellation, Draco the Dragon. Although the Draconic meteor shower was at its apex on the night of October 9, 1992, the Peekskill fireball arrived from the South and therefore was not a Draconid.

It would be extremely difficult to overstate the significance of this. It may be the most important single "message unit" contained in this interworld communication. My reason for why this is important runs as follows:

Draconids get their name from the *northern* constellation, Draco the Dragon. Draco, also spelled Dracon, was also an infamous Athenian archon in the 7th century BC known for his cruel and unusual laws and punishments. Indeed, the word *draconian* enters the human lexicon because of the singular cruelty of these punishments. I don't think we need to go into the details of this ruler's cruelty here, but we should take comfort from the inferrable fact that the dispatchers went to a lot of trouble to find and requisition a one ton *sporadic* meteor that night. Maybe there were no Draconids available the Peekskill meteor's size that night. Whatever the case, the dispatcher(s) of the Peekskill meteor clearly chose *not* to occasion the same sort of *faux pas* with their preemptive rejoinder as NASA chose to occasion and execute three days later. Dr. Mencke told one "Gannett" reporter: *"When we looked at the crater, it was clear (the meteorite) came from the south...It's likely the 30-pound brown and gray rock came from the annual Draconid meteor shower, which was visible the length of the East Coast on Friday night."*

How fortunate was it that Dr. Mencke and all the newspapers and media were dead wrong about the meteor's source? I'd say it's incalculable.

Higher and deeper

In 2009 I troubled the AMNH again with a request to peruse the museum's archives concerning the Peekskill meteor event. The museum had made an exhibit of both the meteorite and Chevrolet in 1993 in the 77th street lobby for several months. Dr. Prinz had passed away by this time. My basic hope was to learn anything that I might have missed about the event. I was also interested to learn what, if anything, the museum had learned about the meteorite and event during its in-house study of both the 27.3 pound artifact from space and the impact itself.

**1993 Exhibit of the Peekskill meteorite and 1980
Chevrolet Malibu at the American Museum of
Natural History in New York City (77th Street
lobby). Reprinted with permission from AMNH.**

After filling out and submitting a bunch of forms, which included my
full reasons for desiring access to the museum's inner sanctum, the
permission I sought was refused. In fact, the museum did not even
give me the benefit of a written refusal. The appropriate office simply
never responded, not even after I filled out all the forms and sent them
in a second time.

What was *really* strange about this is that the managing head of the
museum's archives is a family friend! It made no difference, though.
I still could not get through that rarefied door. Although my friend
was not the decision maker, one would have thought that the personal
association might have helped, a little. I won't mention his/her name
because his/her dire request during my application process with the
museum was that I not breathe a word of our personal association.
"Tom, please, don't even *mention* that you know me." To be blunt
about it, the museum high-ups, whoever they are, avoided me like the
plague. But then, I often have this effect on piled higher and deeper
(PhD) types.

One of the most frequent objections I hear to my meteor-communication
theory relates to the fact that many hundreds of meteors hit the
Earth every year, as if this were some very important fact. Heck,

many thousands more pea-sized meteors burn up in the atmosphere every year after being seen as "shooting stars." But of all the rocks that fly around in our atmosphere, only about five or six meteors are recovered and then made known to scientists every year. The total number of meteors ranging is size from marbles to basketballs, or larger, that reach the surface of the earth to become meteor*ites* each year is around five-hundred. The reason we do not hear about very many of them on the television news or in our newspapers is because they do not generally make themselves visible at 8 o'clock at night. For geophysical reasons, the great bulk of shooting stars are seen *after* midnight. Another reason we don't hear about many of them is that they generally don't uncork Chevrolet signal-lights, or get exhibited in top natural history museums, or get worldwide tours. The Peekskill meteorite and one 1980 Chevrolet Malibu did, though.

Timing again

Why did the Peekskill event occur at 8 o'clock at night, or 7:49 pm, to be exact? Why, the better for people to see it, my dear -- see it, film it, photograph it, analyze it, and even interpret it.

There was something else implied by the Peekskill fireball, something more biting and sarcastic. 1990 and 1991 were the years of the "Patriot missile." These were the "smart" missiles rolled out during the first Iraq war, the police action that followed Saddam Hussein's invasion of Kuwait. Smart missiles are essentially steerable bombs, equipped with lasers, or other guidance systems. Some even come with television cameras on them. They can hone in on and destroy moving targets in the air or stationary targets on the ground.

Patriot missiles were used to intercept an Iraqi dictator's SCUD missiles enroute to targets in Israel and Saudi Arabia. Who can forget those incessantly aired ten-second videos showing ground-to-air or air-to-ground missiles pitching and twisting like bats out of hell toward Saddam's dastardly SCUDs? Some were destroyed; others were not. They gave a fascinated and horrified world a peek at America's latest technology of war. Over and over these videos were beamed into our televisions; over and over these moving images seeped out into space in every direction at the speed of light. Oh my, what a proud and sick spectacle they must have made.

The Peekskill meteor's reference to these naked displays seems unmistakable. So was the message that came attached: "Hey, you think you're hot? Here's a peek at *our* skill, baby!" (just a *peek*, mind you.)

If showing off our respective and latest push-button weapons of mass-destruction was the *sujet pertinente*, then let's be honest. There's absolutely *no* contest here. Besides, where such displays were concerned, the *coup de grace* was yet to come. ETi's second act or signal would, figuratively speaking, blow the scientific world away.

"A scientific man ought to have no wishes, no affections, - a mere heart of stone." -- Charles Darwin

Six
A string of pearls

Something of quite enormous import *did* happen in 93/3. While many will never know or particularly care that it happened, every astronomer in the world knows it well, though many of them today might be hard-pressed to tell you exactly when it all went down. To this day, however, practically no one knows *why* it happened.

Comet Shoemaker-Levy 9 was first spotted on the night of March 24, 1993 by the comet-hunting team of Drs. Carol & Eugene Shoemaker and David Levy. It was found in a photograph taken with the 0.4 meter (1.3 ft) Schmidt telescope at the Palomar Observatory, which stands 5,500 feet above sea level on Palomar Mountain in North San Diego County, California. The comet's discovery was made while conducting a program of observations designed to uncover "near earth objects" in local space, and was formally announced in the International Astronautical Union Circular (IAUC) on March 27, 1993. It was the team's ninth shared comet discovery. They would go on to discover four more together in subsequent years.

Comets don't just happen, they happen along, or they happen to -- planets, moons, planetoids or whatever gets in their way. They can be spotted, observed and tracked, even predicted, but little else can be done with them at this point...unless you happen to be able to control them like so many precious toys. That Shoemaker-Levy 9 was requisitioned, directed and aimed at Jupiter, the largest terrestrial target in the solar system, is predicated on the Peekskill meteor's intelligent auguring of the comet, and on the facts surrounding the earlier impact event, when one of the solar system's smallest targets was tagged within a centimeter of its life. That there was this continuum of magnitudes there can be no doubt. What's more, the comet, dubbed The String of Pearls, turns out to be aptly named because, like Peekskill, it spoke eloquently and powerfully to mankind's past, present and future.

Now, there is nothing quite like 21 small *comets* to augur the 21st century. But then, comets have always been thought to predict major future events on Earth. These wandering planetoids made of ice (H2O) and dust have fascinated or frightened people of all cultures for millenia. The only difference this time was the gods, or whomever, were letting us know quite a bit more than usual. This is not to contend, however, that all previous comets observed in the past were messages from ETi.

So this was what the license plate numbers, 933, portended. Here was that "something" that I knew must be coming in March 1993. And, what a fitting follow-up to the Peekskill fireball-string it was. In a sense, SL9 was Peekskill's mirror, only much bigger, since certain photos of each string set side by side are somewhat difficult to distinguish.

Can there be any real doubt that both meteor-strings (strings!) were, in fact, acts of ETi, and not of unassisted nature? The reason for this may not be one-hundred percent conclusive, but the conclusion is wise, because the glaring fact of the matter is that we don't really have a choice but to make some reading of the chalk here. The sheer destructive power of Shoemaker-Levy 9 makes it imperative for us to not be wrong about who or what really actually dispatched this comet. Since everything certainly points to SL9 and Peekskill being intelligently crafted, it would be stupid to insist on deductive certainty when our very survival as a species could depend on our receiving any messages they conveyed. Now, SL9 conveyed about as stern a message as it is possible to send: "Better survey your own backyard before surveying anyone else's." At the time, or any time, this seems like pretty good advice for one experienced intelligent lifeform to give to another less experienced one.

Showtime!

The String of Pearls, formally designated D/1993 F2, gave immediate notice of its uniqueness because it showed multiple nuclei in an elongated region about 50 arcseconds long and 10 wide, an arcsecond being 1/3600 of a degree. When observations began to be made, the comet was about four degrees from Jupiter as seen from Earth. This led astronomers to believe, though it was never proven, that the comet had been orbiting Jupiter, and not the sun, for some time, probably since the 1970s or mid-1960s, when Jupiter will have captured the parent comet from its original solar orbit. But this becomes sheer astronomical speculation in light of the facts already discussed. A re-examination of several images of the Jovian neighborhood taken before its discovery date showed faint images of the comet-string, including one on March 15, 1993, one on March 17, and a few on the 19th, but no precovery images earlier than March were ever found. This suggests that SL9 was *nowhere* to be found earlier than 93/3.

NASA photo of comet Shoemaker-Levy 9 enroute to Jupiter

That there is this vacuum of evidence about a comet that supposedly broke apart in a previous close *(Roche limit)* pass of Jupiter on July 7, 1992, begs at least two questions: just where did the *string of pearls* actually come from, and, how did it come to be pulled apart into twenty-one pieces? Moreover, why is there is no photographic record of this happening -- I mean, how do you *miss* a thing like that? But if SL9 *did* shatter into its pieces on July 7, 1992, as astronomers confidently asserted, then (guess what?) this was exactly ninety-three (93) days or three (3) months *before* Peekskill went down. 93/3.

Of far more interest to astronomers and scientists in many disciplines than any possible ETi communication was the show about to unfold in the form of twenty-one explosions on Jupiter (an understatement because astronomers and scientists showed *no* interest in my theory). Now, there's hardly anything in the world scientists like more than to watch really, *really* big explosions. Here for the very first time terrestrial scientists were being treated to a spectacle the likes of which they had never seen, or dreamed of seeing, that of solar system bodies colliding. As it happened, the explosions would even be visible to backyard hobby astronomers with telescope apertures of not much mo re than 2 inches. The comet's fragments measured from a few hundred meters to several kilometers in diameter.

**Fragments of comet Shoemaker- Levy 9 impacting
Jupiter from July16-22, 1994. NASA photo.**

Fragment A slammed into Jupiter at 20:13 UTC (3:13 pm EST) on July 16, 1994, at a speed of thirty-seven miles a second. The impact explosion created an ejecta plume that reached a height of 3,600 miles above the giant planet, almost half the diameter of Earth! When the world saw the big dark spot form on Jupiter, the astronomical community became ecstatic. Needless to say, if such an impact were to occur on Earth, the damage would be, well, off the chart.

Over the next six days, the remaining twenty fragments smashed into Jupiter with extensive media coverage. The twenty-one collisions were denoted A through W in the order of their impact, with letters I and O not used. This works out to 21 impacts in all. One of the PBS stations did the "24/7" thing by inviting panels of scientists into their studios to watch and discuss each impact.

Astronomers had approximately sixteen months, from March 24, 1993 to July 16, 1994, to track, study, and watch the String of Pearls perform their final dance, and to prepare for the astronomical show of a lifetime, or many lifetimes. Talk about your cosmic drumroll!

Interestingly, all of the impacts occurred on the *back* side of Jupiter, which reminds us of where the Peekskill meteor struck sixteen months earlier. This is to say, the explosions were not made immediately visible to earth-based telescopes. (Maybe we like explosions a little too much.) Jupiter had to turn on its axis for forty minutes or so before they could be seen. By this time the explosions had had a chance to proliferate quite noticeably in size.

On the other hand, as if to reward us for our deep space efforts, several space-based observatories were able to watch the 21 nuclei of the comet-string plunge into Jupiter as they occurred. These included the Hubble Space telescope, the ROSAT X-ray observing satellite, and the Galileo spacecraft, then on its way to a rendezvous with Jupiter.

The largest impact explosion was fragment G, which occurred July 18. It created a giant spot over 12,000 km (7,200 miles) across, and was estimated to release an energy equivalent to 6,000,000 megatons (six million *million* tons) of TNT, or about six-hundred times the world's entire nuclear arsenal. Two impacts twelve hours apart on July 19 created explosions of similar size as fragment G. The impacts happened one after the other until fragment W struck the planet on July 22.

Jupiter's role as the solar system's cosmic vaccum cleaner became starkly clear with SL9's crash into Jupiter. Being by far the most massive planet in the solar system, it is believed the planet's intense gravitational pull leads about 5,000 times more comets and asteroids to collide with the planet than collide with Earth. Previous Voyager missions to Jupiter have revealed thirteen crater chains on Callisto, one of Jupiter's moons, and three on Ganymede. This compares with one crater chain known to exist in South America where an asteroid (or comet) seems to have bounced on the surface of the Earth at some time within the last ten (or fifty?) thousand years. It has been estimated that comets 0.3 km in diameter impact Jupiter once in approximately 500 years, and those 1.6 km (0.99 mi) in diameter once every 6,000 years or so. By comparison, the comet-string's parent was estimated to be between two-and-a-half and three miles in diameter.

For me, though, none of this mattered so much as the fact that 21 -- not 12, not 18, not even 1 -- cometoids impacted Jupiter. Since comets are known to augur things, too, the hidden in plain view fact of it was that Shoemaker-Levy 9 was auguring the *21st century,* at the time but six years away. Like eloquent pearls, they heralded not just a new century but a brand new millennium. As a lifelong science fiction buff, reading about what the next one-thousand years could bring has to be one of my very favorite things to do.

Dr. Eugene Shoemaker

With his co-discovery of Shoemaker-Levy 9, Dr. Shoemaker soon became a legend among geologists. On SL9's cue, this astro-geologist suddenly became world famous for practically inventing the science of terrestrial impacts. He was the first to observe visual similarities between certain large craters on Earth and nuclear ground explosions, which exhibited in common a marked uplifting of rock at both of their centers. This characteristic formation was also later observed in impact craters on the moon. From this he induced that the terrestrial craters were, in fact, meteoritic impacts -- not extinct volcanos, or some other geologic formation, as had been thought.

Going to the moon had always been Eugene Shoemaker's fondest dream, but in 1963 he was diagnosed with Addison's disease, a condition that prevented him from becoming an astronaut. Although mostly sidelined by the geological establishment before the appearance of SL9, Shoemaker's theories received a large measure of attention and acceptance after it appeared. Since then he has been called the father of the science of near-earth objects.

When the USGS Center of Astrogeology was founded in Flagstaff in 1965, Dr. Shoemaker was appointed its chief scientist. At this time he organized the geological activities planned for the lunar landings. By 1970 he became interested in extending his geological knowledge of terrestrial and lunar impact craters to the study of the astronomical objects that formed them. With Eleanor "Glo" Helin, prinicpal investigator of the Near Earth Asteroid Tracking (NEAT) program of NASA's Jet Propulsion Laboratory, Dr. Shoemaker developed a plan to search for some of these objects (the Apollo asteroids) with the 0.46 meter Schmidt telescope at Palomar. This search program had its first success in July 1973 and was soon significantly augmenting the rather meager knowledge that had been accrued on these objects during the previous four decades. Together with the other observing programs at Palomar, the Shoemakers made the Palomar Observatory the leading site for th e discovery of asteroids. More than 13 percent of asteroids that have been numbered have been found there.

Before comet Shoemaker-Levy 9 was discovered in 93/3, the prevalent theory of geologic formation was uniformitarianism. This theory of dynamic geology states that geologic formations are the result of processes taking millions of years to bring about. It holds that that physical, chemical, and biologic processes now at work on and within the Earth have operated with general "uniformity" through immensely long periods of time and are sufficient to account for all geologic change. This concept was first advanced in 1785 by the Scottish geologist James Hutton in his book <u>Theory of the Earth</u>, and then further expounded in 1802 by another Scotsman, John Playfair, in <u>Illustrations of the Huttonian Theory</u>. This theory was in direct opposition to the previously held theory of catastrophism, which holds that at intervals in the earth's history all living things have been destroyed by cataclysms (e.g., floods or earthquakes) and replaced by entirely different populations.

The debate between these two theories continues to this day, although recent thinking seeks a synthesis of the two theories . With SL9's discovery and subsequent crash into Jupiter, however, the pendulum of belief has swung toward catastrophism, or to what is now called neo-catastrophism.

What is interesting about this old debate is how it derives from an even older rivalry, the one between religion and science. As we saw in chapter one, this antagonism began in earnest with Copernicus, Bruno and Galileo. The theory of uniformitarianism, which science prefers, tends to refute, some say disprove, biblical chronologies and doctrine, which support the main thrust of catastrophism. The truth appears to include both theories, since both geological processes share in the work of terra-forming our planet.

Perhaps the most important thing to come from the recent reformulation of this debate, however, is it immediately improves the outlook for human survival in the face of these outer space objects. You can't do anything about asteroids if you don't know a good deal about them, and what better or surer way was there to incite and improve our understanding of cosmic reality than to provide the two highly accessible and tangible instances of meteor impact events?

The extinction of the dinosaurs at the end of the Cretaceous period is widely believed to have been caused by the impact event that created the Chicxulub crater, more than 110 miles in diameter, in the Yucatán Peninsula in Mexico. As Eugene Shoemaker was so fond of saying, "Yes, Virginia, comets do impact planets."

Shortly before Dr. Shoemaker died in a car crash in Australia in 1997, he said, "Not going to the Moon and banging on it with my own hammer has been the biggest disappointment in life." In death he received his wish by becoming the first person to be buried on another planet. When the tiny Lunar Prospector spacecraft crashed into a dark crater near the Moon's south pole, it deposited onto the lunar surface the ashes of the pioneering astro-geologist. It was a fitting tribute to a great scientist.

"Dare to think! " -- Immanuel Kant

Seven
Hanging up on the Universe

The scientific community was more or less unanimous in its dismissal of my interpretation of the Peekskill and Jupiter impact events. Apparently, no amount of "circumstantial" evidence was going to be enough to pique their interest in my theory. My evidence was seen as anecdotal, unreplicable, unscientific, even as numerology. The endlessly curious nature of the Peekskill event -- its timing, conspicuity, meaningful coincidences, uncanny precision and other facts -- simply could not break through the wall that is science. And, yet, every intuitive cell in my brain was screaming that they were all wrong, that extremely clever alien minds had indeed fashioned *both* impact events.

I wrote to several SETI astronomers at NASA and science journal editors but the response was always the same -- thanks, but no thanks. Yet absolutely nothing they offered in the way of rebuttal impressed me in any way. Their arguments against my theory seemed weak and irrelevant in every instance, as I will attempt to show in this chapter.

It became very clear that the investigators at Ames Research Center and JPL were not really serious investigators of ETi at all, because every detective in the world, especially one with no initial clue as to whom they were looking for, has to rely on circumstantial evidence in order to solve a case. Perhaps instead of Enrico Fermi, Sherlock Holmes should be NASA's guide, the fictional sleuth who advised: *"Never theorize before you have data. Invariably, you end up twisting facts to suit theories, instead of theories to suit facts."*

In 1985, an earth and space science professor known for his theories on extraterrestrials, Dr. James Deardorff, wrote:

> "Were the extraterrestrials to communicate with us via radio waves from space, or via a probe sent to broadcast while circling the Earth, strenuous attempts would no doubt be made by the governmental agency concerned with national security of the country detecting the communications to keep them top secret. It would be quite naive to reason otherwise. The secrecy would be in hopes of obtaining some military or economic advantage over other nations from the decoded information, especially over other nations deemed unfriendly. Even if the detection of the incoming communications by a non-government research group were announced over the news media, the government could easily disclaim it as an erroneous report or a hoax the next day."

> *"ET Strategy for Earth", Quarterly Journal of the British Astronomical Society, 1985.*

I received the article in which this rather sagacious observation appears from the Ames Research Center as part of its response to my apprising the space agency of my findings. I contacted Dr. Deardorff at the University of Oregon to apprise him of my theory and findings, and to congratulate him for this advanced and apparently correct, thinking.

If, as Dr. Deardorff points out in his article, extraterrestrials have educated themselves about the secret games that governments play, and if their intention was to send an overture of greeting to all the people of Earth, then surely they would know better than to attempt this using radiowaves, a technology that is probably ridiculously primitive by their standards in any case. Surely, they would find another way, a way that was government secrecy *proof.*

When the story of Shoemaker-Levy 9 broke in late March of 1993, I immediately knew that this was the very thing I had beeen waiting for. It proved to me beyond any shadow of a doubt that I was right, not only about the license plate numbers being a date, but about my whole theory. SL9 was spectacular vindication and proof that the car and its license plate were the potending vehicles of a message dispatched by superior nonhuman beings.

Believing SL9's intelligently directed crash into Jupiter to be off the chart, I felt it my civic duty to let *someone* know that ETi was now aiming comets at targets in our solar system! Although this was the perceived fact of the matter, I did not make this the subject or tenor of my unsolicited report. I saw the train of comets as extremely beneficial in terms of our previously naiive, but now much improved, understanding of current cosmic reality. But I did strongly suggest that unlike Peekskill, the dispatchers were not exactly playing games this time. The obvious fact of the matter was they were damned serious about what they had tried to impart five months earlier.

I sent a package of information with my observations to NASA-Ames in April 1993, a month after the comet-string Shoemaker-Levy 9 was spotted in March. Of course, I had to apprise NASA of the Peeksksill event's role in predicting the comet. This meant explaining about the license plate of the impacted car with its over-scored numbers, 933 (93/3). I didn't imagine this would go over very well with them, but since it was the key to everything, I had to do it. Aside from pointing out the historical belief about comets and fireballs auguring things, I mentioned the fact that Shoemaker-Levy 9 was basically a copy of the Peekskill fireball, only larger. In fact it's rather hard to tell them apart when viewing side by side photos of them.

The articles I received from Ames Research Center in response seemed encouraging at first blush, but aside from a few interesting facts of which I had not been previously aware, I learned nothing new from them. I was already fairly well aware of the current thinking on ETI. I had made it a kind of life-long study. After reading through the materials I was left with a distinctly unsatisfied feeling. Ames offered no opinion on my findings and theory; their package amounted to a boiler plate response that anyone showing written interest in the center's activities might receive.

By the end of April '93, I had still not seen or heard anything in the press or media to lead me to believe that anyone but myself had perceived the alien overture. No link had been made between the Peekskill and Jupiter impact events. ETi had not been mentioned once in connection with either event. This was when the notion that the events might have been intentionally designed to be unacceptable to SETI scientists really took hold of me. It was now clear that ET's cosmic stimuli had, in fact, meticulously *controlled* for scientists. Heck, if even Deardorff couldn't appreciate my logic, then the designers of Peekskill and SL9 *really* knew their stuff, or at least their human scientists, anyway.

As I mentioned earlier, practically all the scientists to whom I communicated my observations and theory rejected it. These included George Musser, editor of "Mercury" magazine; Carl Sagan of TV-series "Cosmos" fame; Dr. James Deardorff, a retired professor at Oregon State University; David Hughes, editor of the Quarterly Journal of the Royal Astronomical Society; Seth Shostak with NASA's Ames Research Center; Dr. Bernard Haisch, editor of "The Journal of Scientific Exploration"; and, most recently, space scientist/science fiction author, David Brin.

I also mailed or e-mailed what must have been well over a hundred other letters and press releases to the media. Most did not reply. Of those few that did there was the standard reply, something like: Oh, *thank* you for your... information, but so sorry, can't touch this. In other words, thanks, but no thanks. Of those scientists and editors that did reply with reasoning arguments against my theory, it is possible to ascribe certain similarities of thinking.

In early 1996, I wrote an article about the Peekskill and Jupiter impact events and submitted it to Dr. David Hughes at the University of Sheffield's Department of Physics. He, himself, had written a small article in "Nature" magazine about the Peekskill fireball. I figured at least he would have some interest in the subject. The terse reply to my submission follows:

July 2, 1996

Dear Mr. Hackney:

Many apologies about the delay with your paper, unfortunately the referees report arrived when I was in hospital.

I am afraid that the paper has been found to be unsuitable for publication in the *Quarterly Journal.*

Yours sincerely,

David W. Hughes

I was hardly surprised by the Journal's rejection of my submitted paper. "Nature" is one of the more prestigious scientific journals in the world, its publication going back to the 19th century. Of course, I had tried to couch my "data" in terms more or less appropriate for scientific review, but (alas!) this proved impossible given the circumstantial and *ad hoc* nature of my data. The referee's report was not included with the letter.

Another rejection letter for the same article came from the editor of "The Journal of Scientific Exploaration." This response was more in formative, even helpful.

Dr. Bernard Haisch, "Journal of Scientific Exploration":

Dear Mr. Hackney:

I apologize for the amount of time this referee's report has taken. It turns out that the referee was delinquent because he/she was out of the country on extensive leave.

Enclosed is the referee's report on your paper, "The Right Signal"." Based on this report, I regret to inform you that I cannot accept your paper for publication in *Journal of Scientific Exploration*. Perhaps it could be used in Topher Cooper's column, "Anomoly Notes." Feel free to send it for his review if you are interested.

Included with the letter was the referee's report. Finally, I thought, I'd get a scientifically reasoned critique.

Here is that referee's report:

"Basically the paper, "The Right Signal," is well written, with good use of language and well organized. It would make an interesting piece for Reader's Digest or some other popular magazine. The science is basically non-existant. Thomas Hackney supposes that because the meteor hit the rear fender of a car that "it" was sending a message. First, the meteor has to hit somewhere. That it was the fender of a car instead of the roof of a house or the side of a barn or the middle of a road or any of the other specific locations that it could hit is not significant. Now if all fragments of the meteor hit car fenders, or if every meteor fall for a year hit car fenders, that would be different. Even assuming that it did convey a message,

how are we to know what message it was. The author notes one or two possibilities, but gives no reason why they would consitute the message rather than many other equally possible messages. The last time a star was involved in "sending a message" it was to announce the birth of a baby in the middle east. Think how many babies were born in the world on the day of the meteror fall. It could have been announcing one of their births for all we know. Obviously, this is not a paper for JSE. On the other hand it is a well written piece and is interesting to read. It just isn't science."

Let's go over this point by point, shall we?

1. *The science is basically non-existant.*

This statement may well be true. I don't really know what I was thinking when I submitted an article like mine to a scientific journal like JSE. It helps to have "PhD" after your name. It's true, mine does not.

If I remember, my paper attempted to compare what I called *articulate coincidences* with randomly generated data. Was this not scientific? Or is it unscientific to postulate circumstantial coincident details as ET-caused in the first place? From a purely scientific standpoint, it probably was.

Nonetheless, it is an act of pure naivete to use *logical positivism* as the only method for detecting sapient extra-solar beings. If ETs exist, they should be expected to exhibit *intelligent* behavior, which means they will possess agendas, motives, personalities and feelings all their own. Because they will have good reason for not offering up *conclusive* proof of their existence, will it not be necessary to expand the investigative envelope just a bit?

2. *Thomas Hackney supposes that because the meteor hit the rear fender of a car that "it" was sending a message.*

I should first like to mention that the quotation marks around the word "it" are those of the referee, not your author. With this out of the way, I believe my article made it quite clear -- though perhaps not clear enough -- that the meteor, itself, wasn't sending a message, the dispatcher-aimer was. This is just a cheap shot right off the bat, and we can already guess where this critique is going. By suggesting that I, a non-PhD (ergo fool), believe meteors have brains with which to send a message, reveals the referee's *a priori* contempt for my theory, or perhaps to any theory proposed by someone without the letters, PhD, after his name. No, meteors *themselves* do not have any brains with which to send a message, nor do bullets or arrows or even guided missiles. Highly advanced extraterrestrials do, though.

Very much in line with the looseness shown by this referee's *call* was her lackadaisical reading of my paper. I refer to the fact that one of the more important facts to suggest my theory was that the meteor did *not* hit the car's fender; that is, the meteor in question was a fender-neglector, *not* a fender-bender. It is plain to see that while the 4 x 23-inch tail-light was pulverized from one end to the other, both fender and accent were left substantially intact or unphased.

3. *That it was the fender of a car instead of the roof of a house or the side of a barn or the middle of a road or any of the other specific locations that it could hit is not significant. Now if all fragments of the meteor hit car fenders, or if every meteor fall for a year hit car fenders, that would be different.*

Why, indeed. My question is, why would *any* of this be "different?" What proof of intelligent causation would a repetition of this event provide? None. The odds of this would be even more astronomical, to be sure, but how much more astronomical would this be than what actually happened but once? When the odds of an event reach into the many billions to one, as Peekskill did, how astronomical does it need to be before it acquires "significance?" (We'll see this one again.)

4. *Even assuming that it did convey a message, how are we to know what message it was? The author notes one or two*

possibilities, but gives no reason why they would consitute the message rather than many other equally possible messages.

One or two possibilities? Try thirty. There are at least six in the license plate alone. Let's review them:

a. *the day of the month the Peekskill meteor impact occurred, October 9, was 3 days before HRMS began its survey, and 3 days before the American Quincentennial.*

b. *the month and year comet Shoemaker-Levy 9 would appear*

c. *the weight of the Peekskill meteorite, 27.3 pounds or 93.3*

d. *Earth's astronomical identification number, which included its Astronomical Unit (A.U.) and relative position vis-a-vis its sun.*

e. *the effect of NASA's pairing of momentous events was equivalent to rather more than the sum of its parts. 3 + 3 = 6 but 3 $\underline{x}$ 3 = 9.*

f. *Comet Shoemaker-Levy 9 allegedly split apart into 21 fragments on July 7, 93 days (3 months) before the Peekskill meteor split apart midway through its flight path.*

How are we to know which one they meant? Well, all of them, of course, which is to say all of them *at the same time*. We are clearly considering an advanced intelligence here, one with an advanced form of communicating in that it has the ability to convey many ideas with astonishingly little. Conveying real-time messages across the stars cannot come cheap, which puts a premium on such things as elegance and pith. It's called getting a bang for your buck.

Considering the amazing degree of skill displayed in the surgical uncorking of a 4 x 23-inch tail-light, there can be no mistaking what *Peekskill* meant, or whose receptivity the signal was meant to beta-test. Right, Ames?

What's remarkable is not what a talking dog says but that it speaks at all, except in this case we're talking about advanced extraterrestrials, not dogs. Fact was, ET had quite a bit to say, and there wasn't much doubt about the meaning of very much of it. These were actions, not electromagnetic beeps, and like the saying goes, actions speak louder than words.

Given the distinct possibility that our planet has already been discovered by sentients out there somewhere in the universe (i.e. not just in our own galaxy), ETi may have felt a need or desire to inform us that our attempt at *eavesdropping* is something of a concern to them. Of course, they had to do this in a plausibly deniable way, for any of a host of reasons. The referee doesn't seem willing to take an extraterrestrial's point of view into consideration. I find this unfortunate.

Ames/JPL's blythe assumptions concerning their hypothetical non-human "targets" are hard to figure. Drake's equation -- which is generally accepted as a logical estimation of the number of intelligent civilizations in our galaxy -- posits as many as ten planets with advanced civilizations originating on them. Ten *different* intelligent life-forms is a lot to consider, much less predict in every case. If any of them are aware of us, they could easily know that humans are an aggressive, corrupt, self-serving, and often violent lot. This could have dictated a particular method of responding.

Dr. George Musser, "Mercury" magazine:

In 1996 Dr. George Musser was editor of "Mercury" magazine, the quarterly publication of the Astronomical Society of the Pacific. This scientific publication purports to "advance science literacy through astronomy." His response to my submitted paper follows.

"It is an interesting hypothesis, but I have to admit that I don't find the reasoning persuasive. Plenty of meteorites fall to Earth and the timing can always be interpreted as special -- coinciding with some political decision, scientific discovery, etc. The fundamental problem is that there is no way to verify whether the hypothesis is true or not. And, even if it could be proven true, it would tell us little about the intelligence that sent the meteor."

This is actually quite typical of the responses I received from many scientific sources -- especially the bit about "plenty of meteorites falling to earth", as if this were some very trenchant fact. Again, let's consider and rebut Dr. Musser's points, one by one, in the order they are made.

1. *"I don't find the reasoning persuasive."*

Okay, this could be due to a lack of skill in writing scientific papers. I am no scientist, to be sure. I'm not sure anymore if I would really want to be a scientist. Too slow and plodding for my taste. Too many politics, too. My only real training in scientific writing and "the method" was that received in the course of gaining my B.A. degree in experimental psychology at the State University of New York at Stony Brook. Not very extensive, I admit, but better than nothing.

Dr. Musser's refusal to be persuaded could also be due to the aliens, themselves, who may have designed their pyrotechnic tracks to be *unpersuasive to scientists."* As I pointed out to him in my reply, the aimers had good reason to hold back on providing the kind of certitude that the physical sciences like to have. Moreover, any attempt to study or confirm the existence of extraterrestrials will necessarily require an appreciation of psychology.

2. *"...the timing can always be interpreted as special."*

Can it really? Pray, do tell. Does he mean as special as a fireball marking and *responding* to man's first big hunt for ETI? I'd sure like to see or hear what these specially interpreted events could be. Given the extraordinary salience of ETi's ripost to NASA's launch of HRMS, I think one would have to wait a very long time before such an ETi/human occasion or opportunity arrived again. Come on George, cut the crap!

Incidentally, NASA's quincentennial activation of HRMS wasn't just something special going on in our world, this was galactic news -- human beings taking their first big leap, as it were. Hey, inquiring minds wanted to know: who the heck are we, anyway?

3. *"The fundamental problem is that there is no way to verify whether the hypothesis is true or not."*

The awe and mystery of it all. Too bad. Aside from the excellent *use* to which this *lack of conclusivity* was put, there is, in fact, every indication that the hypothesis is *true*. The clues made available in Peekskill's case are not only legion but they accrue to quite convincing evidence of intelligent activity, albeit slightly inconclusive proof. When does science *ever* provide conclusive proof for a theory?

Science isn't the only tool humans have to determine if something may be true or not. We do have other modes of investigation and perception that have served our species quite well over the millenia -- like intuition and common sense. When somebody kicks you in the pants, you don't need a scientific investigation to determine that that someone wants to get your attention to the fact that they are not exactly pleased with you or with something that you did. To put this another way, if a person gathers berries in a jungle and hears a twig snap, he or she doesn't laugh the sound off as "merely subjective" or anecdotal -- not if he or she wants to stay in one piece, that is.

4. *"And, even if it could be proven true, it would tell us little about the intelligence that sent the meteor. "*

I beg to differ. Even without definitive proof, much is learned and inferred from and about this intelligence from the *myriad* of staggering details provided. More important than what our cosmic communicants look like, where they come from, or at what radio frequency they happen to transmit from, is what we can infer first about their nature, about their ethical values, technological capabilities, and their implied knowledge of human history, customs and beliefs. There is even information about the code by which they live: they are very careful, for example, not to interfere in our affairs is crucial for our long term survival.

We learn they are not above boasting about their superior marksmanship, which they did by naming their second demonstration, *"Peekskill."*

Except for the lack of scientific method exhibited in my paper, I do not believe he made a single valid point.

Let's now consider another scientific reaction to my observations, this time from a SETI scientist at the Ames Research Center where the SETI Institute is located. Surely, here we'll get a point of view that actually takes the alien point of view into account, right?

Dr. Seth Shostak, Senior SETI Scientist, Ames Research Center (NASA)

Sept. 5, 1998, Sat. 11:47 AM

Dear Tom,

Well, I went to your (web) site. It's nicely laid out. However, I can't believe that you actually think that the chondritic meteor that hit a car in 1992 has anything to do with extraterrestrials, let alone that it might be a signal.

A few obvious points: the meteor's parent body never gets any farther from Earth than 2.1 AU from the Sun. That puts it a bit past Mars. Do you honestly think there are intelligent beings within a few tens of millions of miles? And, if so, that they would "communicate" by sending signals consisting of meteors? There are thousands of meteors that hit the Earth during every 24 hours. The total weight is about a ton or two, daily. To argue this would be like deciding that a piece of driftwood that happened to wash up on the beach and bump into a dozing sunbather 7 months ago was somehow a signal from (a) deep sea intelligence, trying to make a comment about Monica Lewinsky and Bill Clinton.

Another obvious point: The HRMS start date (October 12) was set less than two years before 1992...in 1990, in other words. I know this for a fact, as I was personally involved. Even assuming that this information was broadcast into space immediately (and I don't think it was, but no matter...), that means that no intelligence farther than 1 light-year from Earth would have had time to (1) learn about the October 12 start, and (2) send some "message" back, even assuming they sent it back at the speed of light (which is a lot faster than meteors travel). The nearest star is four times as far. So this makes no sense, unless you think the aliens hang around Jupiter or Pluto or some other neighborhood body...

Yet another point, along the same lines: remember that the HRMS was designed to listen for radio signals from other star systems, typically a hundred light-years away. This is millions of times farther than the asteroids of our solar system. What could possibly be the connection? Why would any neighborly aliens care about radio telescopes trained on the stars?

Do you think the dinosaurs were getting a message 65 million years ago? Or were they simply the victims of a cosmic accident, caused by the continuous bombardment of debris suffered by all the inner planets? If an alien cell phone had dropped onto Peekskill, I would have been impressed. Meteors drop every day. Most of them miss our cars. Some of them won't.

Sincerely,

Seth Shostak

Let's consider Dr. Shostak's "few obvious points." First, that intelligent beings would need to be within a few million miles of Earth in order to dispatch a signalling meteor. Obviously, his disbelief is based on the idea that if an ETi were that close to Earth we would certainly have detected them by now. This assumes a lot. It assumes that our *detecting* technology is on a par with their *stealth* technology. Imagine that! A human technology no more than a few hundred years in the making is going to be able to penetrate their hiding technology which could be many hundreds of millions of years in the making. Actually, this addresses all three "obvious points" raised.

A SETI scientist really ought to have a broader view of what "They" *might* be capable of.

As for the second part of his objection concerning why extraterrestrials would "communicate" by sending signals consisting of meteors, I can think of several good reasons for such an approach. I believe we covered this in chapter three, but let's look at one of these reasons again. Meteors are natural and therefore plausibly deniable. It's quite true that meteors make themselves known all the time, a fact that provides them wonderful cover. As for *why* ETi should want to float a plausibly deniable communication, the reason could also be simple. Maybe it is because they do not we are ready to intermingle with civilized worlds; maybe there is a codex they follow which restricts them from *directly* contacting worlds like ours. As noted earlier, there are many plausible and good reasons for a partial and indirect approach to contacting our world.

Then there is the question: *"Why would any neighborly aliens care about radio telescopes trained on the stars?"* Whether or not ETi gives a hoot about this is not necessarily the main issue here. The issue here is how or *whether* to make contact with us at all. It seems to me that what ETi did to begin or at least broach this process was exceptionally appropriate, if not brilliant.

Here is another reply (there were several in all) from Dr. Shostak some months later.

Dear Mr. Hackney,

Thanks for the e-mail. Well, as I thought I mentioned, the argument you present is numerology and post hoc statistics. I don't think that will find much acceptance in the science community. It doesn't explain anything and it doesn't have any predictive power -- both are hallmarks of science.

Good luck with your new version, however.

Sincerely,

Seth Shostak

I had heard the "numerology" argument before. The allegation is rubbish. If a message happens to be encoded in numbers and symbols that need to be deciphered and interpreted, does this make the deciphering an excercize in numerology? Of course not. The stylus used for the message was indicative of a preference for a particular system or style of communication, one that allowed its sender to broach contact in a plausibly deniable and safe manner. If Dr. Shostak wanted to call my sort of exposition something, he could have called it *semiotics*, inasmuch as it tries to examine certain signs and symbols in terms of their situational context, or *pragmatics*, since it takes into account the communicator's knowledge of the listener's beliefs. But these are linguistic fields that this SETI scientist apparently has no understanding of or use for.

The whole issue here centers around the clear and stubborn fact that the dispatchers of this testing overture were *not* going to provide scientific proof, or anything that would allow scientists or anyone else to gleen their identity, appearance or planet of origin. Providing this kind of intimate and strategic information is apparently not the way it's done. There are protocols to meet and tests to make first. One would think that a SETI scientist would appreciate this, but, (alas!) Dr. Shostak does not. Apparently, strong *hints* do not count, nor does political realism, or creativity, from either the sender or the receiver.

In the scientist's world, such things as proper procedure and protocol, or security through anonymity, can not matter. A scientist understands only two things: control and replicability. If a thing cannot be replicated and controlled, if it occurs only once, it is pretty much irrelevant.

It appears that no real thinking was going on at the SETI Institute regarding intelligent extraterrestrials. I wrote similar e-mails and letters to several other Ames Research Center/SETI Institute staff members, including Dr. Jill Tarter, an HRMS project chief. I received no reply from any of them.

Dr. David Brin, author:

The idea finally occurred to me to contact a scientist who is also a science fiction author. Surely, I would get some more sophisticated thinking on the subject. David Brin is the author of sumerous science fiction novels such as his "Uplift" series. He is also a media pundit, public speaker, and technical consultant, and advisor to committees dealing with subjects as diverse as national defense, astronomy and space exploration, SETI and nanotechnology.

Here is one response I received from him in 2010 after contacting him for his views about a three-part documentary video I made about my ETi discovery.

Thomas,

Thanks for your note and remarks.

As for your 933 hypothesis, I must tell you that I bridge every angle you'd want from an outsider... both scientist and wildly speculative science fiction author. And alas I find the whole thing lacking from every angle.

(Mind you, you have a really cool-sounding voice and manner in the films and a very amiable presentation.)

I cannot swallow the logic from ANY of the angles I come from. Even as a story, you create a case based on ONE incident! Please Thomas, that's disappointing, even for an alien-mystery scenario. You then create a strawman, that "scientists" poohpooh interstellar travel, which is nonsense. A great many of us know full well (and better than you, in fact) that IS travel is possible and indeed a constraint on the Fermi Paradox.

Look, I don't want to offend a fan and one who is clearly bright and talented. But there are so many flaws... and the worst is that you contend aliens would offer up a hint... to you. Since you are the one to notice. And not go any farther or offer anything else to anybody else.

That is called solipsistic exceptionalism and it derives from wishful perception. Moreover, even if it were true... that would make the ETs really really lame... total dorks. Beings not worth my time.

Essentially, you are talking about "lurkers" and I have explored the idea in great detail. See: http://ieti.org/articles/brin.htm

I consider such creatures worthy of only one thing. To be snubbed.

Wish I had time for extended exchanges. I don't. But stay vivid and creative!

With cordial regards,

David Brin

http://www.davidbrin.com

Well, I do not really have "a cool-sounding voice"; I have never liked it. Amiable? Maybe, but this is truly irrelevant. More to the point is: "...the worst (flaw) is that you contend aliens would offer up a hint... to you. Since you are the one to notice. And not go any farther or offer anything else to anybody else."

The philosophy of solipsism states that only the self exists, or can be proven to exist. In point of fact, both are true statements, since groups (of selves) are an abstraction. Only the individual brain exists. There is no collective brain or entity in this Earthly mileau. So solipsistic exceptionalism, as he calls it, is really just another word for individualism, and of this I am happy to be and remain.

That I was the only one to *inform* him of the information can not be a basis for saying, or charging, that I was "the only one to notice." The point he makes is a *non sequitur*, though, a head game. Absolutely anyone could have noticed what I noticed. It could have been David Brin, it could have been someone else. It just turned out to be me *(blimey!)*.

As noted previously, strict scientific thinking may have been *purposely* controlled for as a kind of joke. If it was, it is a joke someone like Dr, Brin may never get.

None of this really matters, though. What matters is that the signals are now able to be laid out and discovered by everyone. The evidence stands on its own multiple (?) feet. But, if there is some big secret about detecting ETi, its a pretty simple one: dare to consider *their* point of view.

Next we come to the *three* little incidents, not just one, as Brin misstates. (We'll tackle the third impact event in the series shortly.) I certainly hope that three incidents will not be too disappointing to him, should he ever bother to fully apprise himself of my observations.

The point Brin makes about the ET being really lame and dorky seems lame. (dorky?) To be honest, I don't think this particular ETi likes scientists like him very much, either. Consider the sport that was made of those birds of a feather calling themselves SETI "investigators." It was as if to say, *"Better leave <u>no</u> stone unturned in your search for ETi. No blinders here, my friend."*

Brin may have me, though, on the "straw-man" issue. I always used to hear scientists pooh-pooh interstellar travel. Have they changed so much? Well, I'm not sure. I am sure that many of the scientists he contends with on a daily basis are beyond the "space is too big" thing, but what about the majority who are not connected with SETI? What about those legions of scientists that will have nothing to do with aliens, or SETI, or anything of this "silly" kind?

All insults of men and aliens aside, facts are facts. A meteor *did* take out a car's signal-light in Peekskill three days before HRMS *was* commenced on the Quincentennial. A 21-car comet-train *did* impact Jupiter. They stand etched in recorded and scientific history. They are not going away.

Dr. Carl Sagan, Cornell University:

Shortly before he died, Dr. Sagan received a letter from me containing some of the key observational data found in this book. I admit to a certain thrill in receiving his letter in response. He wrote:

"You have failed to make the crucial distinction between *a priori* and *a posteriori* statistics."

Unfortunately, I have lost the letter that came on Cornell University stationary, but this was basically all he wrote, other than a phrase of thanks for sending my material. I racked my brain trying to figure out what he was driving at here, but I'm afraid the point eludes me to this day (I think this was his intention). Frankly, I don't see that statistics, *whether a priori* or *a posteriori*, has very much to do with anything here. Because the signal-carrying events were on time, on target, and on topic, I believe they transcend statistics. ETi cannot be logically deduced from the events in question. It seems ETi *prefers* to be only logically *induced*, or intuited, at this time, which as have already noted made good sense from their perspective.

True investigators of ETi would have at least *considered* this evidence in light of their historical timing. Any detective worth his or her salt would laugh at the idea of denying circumstantial evidence. There is not a detective in the world who has not relied on it heavily to solve a case. Besides, there is the sneaking suspicion (intuition) that a discovery of this magnitude would *not* come in the precise fashion expected.

So what came of HRMS? Was the federal project really just another waste of government money, 100 million dollars worth? The freshman Senator from Nevada, Richard Bryan, seemed to think so. A 1993 press release from his office said:

"The Great Martian Chase may finally come to an end. As of today, millions have been spent and we have yet to bag a single little green fellow. Not a single martian has said 'take me to your leader,' and not a single flying saucer has applied for FAA approval."

It's funny how the truth will get you every time when you make blithe statements like this. Yes, HRMS, alias SETI, was shut down, defunded, and run out, by the end of 1993, after only one year of operation. Great was the disappointment at NASA-Ames and JPL. SETI sustained a major setback, and basically went bust for many years.

Actually, the good senator and his cohorts might have saved the country about three million dollars a year over the remaining nine years the project was originally funded for (big deal). NASA had already spent upwards of 65 million dollars on development of the alien-hunting system and for one year of operation. It's almost embarrassing to say how "highly" some people think of our extraterrestrial neighbors. SETI's sinking was, of course, one of the final ironies of the whole thing.

One last question: Was HRMS shut down because SL9 accurately predicted appearance all but *confirmed* my theory regarding its intelligent cause? Did it suddenly become too danger to pooh-pooh? Defunding HRMS may have been the government's way of "getting the message." Somehow, I doubt this, but you never know what secretive governments are up to these days.

Logic dictates truth, and the truth here is there can be no real doubt that our world *has* been visited by conscious entities slightly beyond our world. Let's cut the crap. These articulating coincidences are NOT coincidences. ETi is here.

"When you enter a room, you have to kiss his ring. I don't mind, but he has it in his back pocket." -- Don Rickles on Frank Sinatra

Eight
Miscellaneous Science!

In the previous chapter, Dr. George Musser tells us: "Plenty of meteorites fall to Earth and the timing can *always* be interpreted as special -- coinciding with some political decision, scientific discovery, etc." Is this really true? I don't think so.

What was happening in the Western world on October 12, 1992 really was special, a lot more special than some industry-written piece of legislation being rubber-stamped (and unread) by congress, or an obscure scientific discovery being made. One could even call the date momentous, or doubly momentous, if you want to include that first

official search for sentient extra-solar intelligence. The hands of the BIG clock were being reset that day, in more ways than one.

I wonder what Dr. Musser would have thought if a meteor had crashed right smack in the middle of the Ames Research Center's front door at 12:01 P.M. on October 12, 1992. Of course, I also wonder what the SETI investigators at Ames research Center would have thought about such an occurrence. Would anyone there have thought that something was a little more than just odd about this? Surely some would have thought so, but whether or not they would keep the errant thought to themselves for fear of being tagged an ET-nut is hard to say. There could be no *scientific* reason or excuse to justify such a leap, for what sure proof would there be for extraterrestrial involvement in this perfectly natural meteorfall? Zero.

Like Peekskill, any thought of extraterrestrial messaging would have to be thrown out as anecdotal, unreplicable, and unscientific. That's science for you. The problem, of course, would be that of *data selection bias*. NASA could only be interested in, was only set up to receive, *radiowaves*, not meteors, or anything else.

Dr. Musser was right about one thing, though. Of all the tidings, commentary, intimations and predictions blazoned that night, the fireball's *timeliness* was the most indispensable. Without the commencement of HRMS the following Monday, whether in conjunction with the Columbian quincentennial or not, there could have been no ready-made opportunity to interject a reply to what was going down on the twelfth. In fact, it's hard to pick any date in human *history* more evocative of ETI than October 12, 1992. So if an ETi were ever going to broach contact, the occasion of mankind's first *official* and major search for ETI was the ideal occasion. By choosing to send on the *9th* of October, this allowed just enough time for the news media, government, NASA, and general public to form some reaction to the event in the few remaining days to October 12. Full reception of the overture by NASA could have been signaled by the project being postponed by a day, if only to avoid the *faux pas* of activating a search for "new worlds" on the Quincentennial Columbus day.

A default message

The information provided by Peekskill/Shoemaker matters. Indeed, our survival as a species could depend on our heeding the warnings it contained. Comets can *cause* extinction, as they have many times during the long history of our planet.

Conversely, a comet or asteroid also allowed for the *rise* of human beings, after it killed off the reigning dinosaurs 65 million years ago. Comets, for their part, plant the seeds that create life. They provide a planet with water, nitrogen, phosphorous, amino acids, and maybe even some bacteria. They are the wandering Johnny Appleseeds of the universe. Both the Peekskill fireball and its comet-string followup became wonderful and apt metaphors for NASA's, or any, search for life.

That geological science would not come to accept Eugene Shoemaker's geological theory of *catastrophism* until Shoemaker-Levy 9 impacted Jupiter provides stark proof of the importance of Shoemaker-Levy 9 in reshaping our understanding of the cosmos. The beauty and power of Peekskill/SL9 was that scientists did not even need to relate these impact events to extraterrestrials in order to *receive* this message.

Once intelligent life takes root on a planet, its long-term survival will depend on its ability to intercept the path of comets and asteroids. If a way is not found, the life will eventually be extinguished by a comet or large asteroid. It is simply a matter of time. If, on the other hand, a resident intelligence does achieve the ability to alter cometary and asteroidal paths, it buys itself more time, time that might be used to colonize other planets or overcome the many technical difficulties of space travel, both of which greatly increase a species' chances to survive and evolve longitudinally.

These were the facts of life read to us in March, 1993 (93/3).

Regardless of whom or what these impacts were attributed to, the people of Earth received *a* default message. That tacit message was something like --

"Better 'survey' your *own* backyard before surveying anyone else's."

This sounds like pretty sound advice to me. While not as glamorous as searching for or investigating black holes and quasars, comets and asteroids can be said to hold a certain fascination in the brass tacks of human survival department.

As a direct consequence of Shoemaker-Levy, new initiatives were started by space agencies and private groups around the globe to try to locate and track all of the many thousands of asteroids that populate our orbital region of the solar system. As for the lay population, a large number of movies and documentaries began to appear about comets and asteroids impacting or threatening to impact the Earth.

From this it would appear that the dispatcher-aimers are quite concerned about us. It simply wouldn't do for a comet to suddenly appear out of nowhere one night and then proceed willy nilly to take our species out, at least not without giving us some initial incentive to develop defenses to protect ourselves from this inevitable occurrence. It seems a small kick in the pants was necessary to wake us up to this dangerous reality.

By offering their signals on the cusp of the American quincentennial, there was the implication of our "coming of age," a theme reinforced by ETi's selection of a meteorite recipient whose 18th birthday just happened to be October 12, 1992. It was as if to relate the fact that it's high time we took a little responsibility for *ourselves,* time for the adolescent to stop looking up and saying "wow" all the time and start doing the things that matter the most, adult things.

As of 2012, almost half of the asteroids thought to exist in the solar system have been identified. It is a good start, perhaps, but comets can appear quite suddenly. At any time a passing star can nudge a comet out of the Oort Cloud or Kuiper Belt, where millions of comets currently reside, and fling it toward the inner planets. It is strange to think that our solar system is literally ringed with frozen water, and it seems a good bet that solar systems that are will have one or more watery worlds.

Until recently, significant progress in asteroid detection had been made by both amateur and professional astronomers, that is, until the

U.S. government effectively shut down the availability of government satellite data in 2009. The U.S. military policy decision explicitly stated that observations by secret government spacecraft of incoming bolides and fireballs are now to be classified "secret" and thus withheld from the public.

For what conceivable reason is this meteoritic data now being withheld from comet-hunting scientists? Now that this important source of meteoritic data has been shut off from the public domain, the scientific community's two decades long asteroid-hunting effort will for lack of data probably eventually come to a close. From now on objects in space will be the exclusive domain of shadow governments and their rulers. One could almost wonder what these unelected agencies and entities intend to do with this information.

NEAR

Before federal satellite went dark to the public in 2009, The Great Comet Crash of 1994 was able instigate a NASA space project called NEAR, the Near Earth Asteroid Rendezvous. NEAR was the first ever closeup study of a near earth asteroid. Eros is one of the largest asteroids in our local space at twenty-one miles long and eight miles wide. The NASA project was renamed NEAR Shoemaker to honor Dr. Eugene M. Shoemaker (1928-1997), the now legendary astro-geologist.

The first in NASA's Discovery Program of low-cost planetary missions, NEAR launched from Cape Canaveral Air Station on February 17, 1996. After a four-year journey that included flybys of Earth (Jan. 1998) and asteroids Mathilde (June 1997) and Eros (Dec. 1998), NEAR began orbiting Eros on Feb. 14, 2000. The car- sized spacecraft observed the asteroid from various distances, coming within several miles of the surface, before the mission ended in February 2001. The Johns Hopkins University Applied Physics Laboratory designed and built the NEAR spacecraft and managed the mission for NASA's Office of Space Science.

NEAR Shoemaker snapped 69 high-resolution pictures of the asteroid during the final few minutes of its descent. They are the closest pictures ever taken of an asteroid, the camera delivering pictures from as close as 394 feet.

Asteroids that come within 121 million miles of the sun are known as near-Earth asteroids. Most of the near-Earth asteroids known are about a half-mile or one kilometer in diameter. So far NASA researchers have found around 350 near-Earth asteroids larger than 1 kilometer in diameter. From this information they estimate that anywhere from 500 to 1,000 similar-sized NEAs are spinning around our solar system, all with specific orbits and velocities. The good news is that none of them will hit Earth anytime soon. The NEAR mission to Eros will help scientists *when* (not if) one of these asteroids (or a comet) bares down on our planet at some time in our future.

The total cost of the NEAR mission was $224 million, or a little more than twice the cost of HRMS.

Science!

Before he passed away in 1998, one of my closest friends was Herbert Bailey.* In 1956 and 1958 Herb wrote two books on the anti-cancer agent, Krebiozen, and the conspiracy perpetrated against it by organized medicine. Herb in his younger days was a Chicago newspaperman whose main beat was promising medical research and breakthroughs. One of these breakthroughs was Krebiozen, a nontoxic chemical found naturally in the body of horses (possibly all animals, it was theorized), that reduced tumor sizes by 50 to 100 percent when injected into the bloodstreams of advanced cancer patients. Among its many observed benefits was relief from pain in far advanced cancer patients, allowing previously bed-ridden patients to walk again and lead more or less normal lives. I am honored to be mentioned in the acknowledgements of his last book, "Vitamin E: for a healthy heart and a longer life." He signed my personal copy of the book with the inscription, "For your loyalty and diligent efforts in our great cause. -- Herb. Nov. 14, 1993 - Also I meant what I said in the acknowledgements."

In the Acknowledgements, he wrote:

" ... Another of my researchers who deserves special credit is Thomas Hackney, who through many years has shown his versatile abilities to ferret out little-known facts."

I considered myself lucky to know and work with Herb. My girl friend at the time, Cathy Hartford, introduced us sometime in 1980. I soon became his beckon-call assistant and loyal friend. Although many of his books are seminal works in the field of vitamin health, you will not find his biography in *Wikipedia*, or anywhere else on the internet. His books are highly suppressed by the medical establishment because they expose a pattern of deceit and hypocricy in organized allopathic medicine. For as long as I knew him, Krebiozen was always the main subject of conversation, what us Lieutenants were supposed to be all about -- i.e. *getting the non-toxic substance Krebiozen back in the news and in the market where it could do some good.*

The only way to do this seemed be to obtain a new batch of the substance. This meant funding. Both a specially equipped lab and horse farm were needed, as well as the scientific expertise to extract the immunological chemical ("K") from the blood serum of horses. I wrote to every foundation I could find. I came closest with billionaire Ross Perot, but when it came down to the nitty-gritty, the funding simply wasn't to be had, from anyone.

The great puzzle of cancer had occupied Krebiozen's discoverer, Stevan Durovic, since his medical school days at the University of Belgrade. In 1933 he obtained a desk at the famed Pasteur Institute in Paris where he pursued his interest in mycology, which is the study of molds, from which penicillin and other life-saving antibiotics have come. Penicillin hadn't been heard of in the 1930s though it was discovered by Dr. Fleming in 1929.

When he became a Professor of Medicine at the University of Belgrade, Dr. Durovic began to investigate why normal cells become abnormal, why they suddenly grow for themselves and not for the benefit of the organism as a whole? He reasoned that all cancers have one thing in common: unregulated growth. If something could be found which negates this common demoninator, there would be your basic cure. He also noted that occasionally a cancer will simply fade away on its own accord, a phenomenon the medical fraternity calls *spontaneous regression*. If he could find that natural control mechanism, that too would be your basic cure for cancer.

It was this immunological "something" that Dr. Stevan Durovic discovered in 1949. Herb Bailey described the Serbian researcher's moment of truth this way:

"One afternoon as he was half-dozing, the fair rich fields of his ancestral estate rolled before his mind's eye, he saw again the familar herds of cows and horses. The answer to his problem came to him! The final answers to most questions are comparatively simple, and this answer was simple -- once you perceived it. Among his father's horses and cows sometimes there appeared a strange disease. It began as a tiny growth, usually on the side of the neck or jaw. Within a few weeks, the growth would burgeon into a huge tumor. The horse would become very sick, often die. Sometimes, however, the horse would recover and the tumor would completely disappear. Surely, this was one of the fastest growing living things composed of animal tissue. It was obvious, too, that when the horse recovered, something in the horse's body had put a halt to the rabid growth by killing the invading cells. All this in a matter of weeks!" *

(* Krebiozen - Key to cancer? Herbert Bailey, Hermitage, 1955)

With some of his family's wealth Dr. Durovic set up a research laboratory in Argentina with the express purpose of finding a cure for cancer. He had been an inmate in an Italian prisoner of war camp while serving as a doctor in the Serbian army; his unit had been captured by the invading German army and sent to the POW camp in Italy. Fortunately for him (and perhaps someday even us), Stevan's first cousin was Queen Helena, wife of the recently deposed Italian monarch, Vittorio Emmanuel. Helena had begged the favor of Pope Pius XII in Rome to intercede for her imprisoned cousin with the Italian authorities. The pope graciously agreed and the pope was subsequently successful in securing Stevan's freedom. Stevan was then allowed to migrate to the neutral country of his choice. Since the United States had three days prior to Helena's interview with Pius declared war on Japan, his second choice, Argentina, became his new and his brother Marko's new home. Stevan immediately began his research. His single-minded goal was to isolate the theoretical substance that occasionally came to a horse's rescue after it came down with "lumpy jaw", and then to see if it would shrink malignant human cancers, as well.

By 1950, Dr. Durovic had found and isolated substantial quantities (a few grams) of the immunological susbstance which horses sometimes produce when afflicted with lumpy jaw. He began testing it on old cancerous dogs. with amazing results. Not only did this natural substance reverse or eliminate the cancers but it also cured the dogs of their cataracts. The next step was to test it on humans. For this he contacted one of the great medicos and cancer researchers in the United States, Dr. Andrew C. Ivy, Vice President of the University of Illinois and head of its huge medical school. Dr. Durovic had read some of his research papers and he knew that Dr. Ivy thought along very similar theoretical lines as he.

To make a long and amazingly detailed story short, Dr. Ivy became Dr. Durovic's greatest ally in what was one of the great medical controversies of the 20th century. Organized medicine was adamantly against Krebiozen and the approximately 200 doctors who were using Krebiozen to treat their patients with advanced cancer. The American Medical Association immediately put out a "study" (in six weeks!) which purported to show that Krebiozen was of no use whatever in the treatment of cancer. This so-called study, known as the "A.M.A.

Status Report" was actually false and bogus, as anyone can discern by reading the debates and proceedings of the Congressional Record (88th congress). The Senator from Illinois, Paul H. Douglas, was one of Krebiozen's greatest proponents.

Despite an independent study involving more than one hundred practicing physicians, which showed Krebiozen in some 5,000 cases to be more efficacious than any *toxic* medication then in use, the F.D.A. banned Krebiozen from interstate commerce in 1964. Adding insult to this worldwide injury, Dr. Durovic was run out of the country, and Dr. Ivy was subjected to a smear campaign by the press. Two uncharacteristically large articles appeared in "Life" magazine (sic), painting Dr. Ivy as this senile dupe of the "secretive Yugoslav", Durovic. The first of them used almost a full page to show a spectrograph which purportedly "proved" that Krebiozen was nothing more than the common body substance, *creatine*. This may have convinced the magazine's millions of lay readers, but like the A.M.A.'s earlier "Status Report" on Krebiozen, the identification depicted was completely bogus. Illinois Senator Paul H. Douglas, speaking to The 88th Congress (1st Session) of the United States, explains why:

"First, the so-called identicle fingerprints are not identicle but there are significant differences throughout at least half the span of the spectrum. Second, chemical analysis demonstrates that Krebiozen is not creatine. Third, the difference in color demonstrates that Krebiozen is not creatine. Creatine is pure white or colorless to the naked eye; it does not fluoresce under ultraviolet light. But Krebiozen is tan to the naked eye and fluoresces under ultraviolet light. Fourth, Krebiozen contains at least six sugars and nine acids not in creatine...

"The Food and Drug Administration did not squarely overlay the two graphs. It dropped one one graph 7-1/2 percent below the other. This obliterates the area of maximum difference between the two graphs. I do not say this was done intentionally. I do say that the result was deceptive, in that it would serve to convince a layman, who did not know

spectrographic analysis of the identity of the two substances (creatine and Krebiozen)."

Taking a serious medical issue and turning it into a human interest story about a "sharp-eyed" 20-year old chemistry student who discovered the spectrographic identification, the F.D.A. promoted the fiction that Krebiozen was a common body substance and therefore, obviously, useless as a treatment for cancer. Of course, no medico or chemist would put their reputation on the line by endorsing the fiction. In this way, Dr. Ivy -- the recipient of five honorary degrees and eleven medical awards, author of 1500 medical papers, the man who at one time or another had served as the A.M.A. Section Chairman for Physiology and Pathology, President of the American Physiological Society, Scientific Director of the National Naval Medical Research Institute, and Director-at-large of the American Cancer Society, the man whom the A.M.A. had selected in 1946 to represent the American medical establishment at the Nuremberg Medical Trials in Germany -- was pilloried and discredited. By this time, Dr. Ivy had already been fired from his position as Vice President of the University of Illinois.

A few attempts were made in 1990s to artificially synthesize the substance from what few samples of krebiozen still existed, but these ended up unsuccessful. The quantity of the krebiozen sample was the main problem, not the chemistry. Funding always seemed just around the corner, rather like the establishment's perrenial claim that the "cure is just around the corner."

In 1991 a ninety-year-old doctor tested Krebiozen on an AIDS patient off-shore (testing "K" on U.S. soil would have been a crime) with several of the last remaining ampules of krebiozen then known to exist. This physician-turned researcher remembered Krebiozen and what had been done to it and everyone connected with it way back in the day. He wrote a letter to Herb, as many other researchers did, to report his findings. Krebiozen was *completely* effective in reversing the AIDS infection of a popular perfomer." The famous patient, whose name I never learned, later died because Dr. Alexander ran out of his small suppy of *Krebiozen*. Needless to say, neither the medical establishment, the media nor it's big pharma sponsors wanted to hear any of that!

Krebiozen production is relatively easy to accomplish. The procedure is straight-forward and laid out in some detail in the notes and testimony of its discoverer. But because it is non-toxic, substantially efficacious, natural, unpatentable, and cheap to produce, the world has been deprived of one of nature's great gifts. As the Congressional Record and "Krebiozen Hearings" also clearly show, the world has been deprived of Krebiozen because in late 1950 Dr. Durovic refused to sell distribution rights to his substance to two Chicago businessmen with whom the A.M.A. treasurer at the time, one Dr. J.J. Moore, was "good friends."

Why do I mention this unfortunate bit of history here? The reason will become self evident in ETi's third and last signal (but the first to happen). This is the subject of the next chapter.

Whatever must happen ultimately should happen immediately.

- Henry Kissinger

Nine
Princeton

Perhaps the strangest of the three ETi-instigated events occurred two days *before* the Peekskill event in a town called Princeton. It occurred on the morning of Wednesday, October 7th, 1992. I don't recall exactly when I first saw the little boxed story in the "Daily News" but it must have been sometime after the 10th of October. The headline was: "Shoots own foot thrice."

It seems a man in Princeton, West Virginia was cleaning his guns on Wednesday morning, Oct. 7, while drinking beer (probably not a good idea *any* time). Below is the AP article as it appeared in the New York "Daily News."

Shoots own foot thrice

Princeton, W. Va. - A man accidentally shot himself three times in the right foot while cleaning three handguns, police said.

The 38-year-old man was drinking beer Wednesday morning when he decided to clean his guns, according to a report filed by Mercer County Sheriff's Deputy L.R. Catron.

His .32-caliber handgun went off, but it "didn't hurt" so he finished cleaning the .32, then began cleaning his .380-caliber pistol, which also went off, said the report.

That bullet "stung a little, but not too bad,"
Catron quoted the man as saying.

The man finished cleaning the .380 and then pulled out his
.357-caliber pistol, only to shoot himself a third time.

The man finally called an ambulance. Catron said the man
told him the .357 shot "really hurt because the bullet was a
hollow point."

I had been searching through all the newspapers I could find for coverage of the Peekskill fireball. There are three major newspapers in New York City, more or less the number you'd expect to find in a town with a population of a hundred thousand or so. Two of these three newspapers -- the "NY Post" and "Daily News" -- carried something about the fireball item. The third NY paper, the "New York Times" had bigger fish to fry, so no coverage was made of the fireball here. Apparently, what happened in the Northeast during the night of October 9, 1992, terminating in Peekskill, 27 miles north of New York City, wasn't news 'fit to print."

The little boxed filler story from Princeton consumed exactly the same amount of space on the "Daily News" page as the Peekskill story, about the size of your minimum two by three-inch display ad. The curious thing about its *placement*, though, was that both the Oct. 7 Princeton story and Oct. 9 Peekskill story ended up on the *same page* of the "Daily News!" This was fortuitous, actually, because if they hadn't been printed on the same page, I probably wouldn't have noticed or thought very much of the Princeton item.

This brings up the question, why and how did *this* happen? I mean, why did everything have to be so *nailed* and in my face? There could be little doubt that whoever read the Peekskill story on the top of the page was probably also going to notice and read the Princeton story at the bottom of the page. As for the question posed above, well, do we really want to go there? Probably not, and unless the reader has a better idea, maybe we'll just go ahead and chalk this one off to dumb coincidence, okay? Hey, it happens. Ah, yes, that's better.

I studied both articles, as I did every other word and story on the page (with the proverbial fine-tooth comb) looking for clues or anything odd. Curiously, the much longer article, which continued to another page, about the results of Guyana's presidential election, was also of unusual interest to me. I had recently supported one of this election's candidates, Dr. Leslie Ramsammy, M.D., for the presidency of Guyana. I had tried, among other things, to raise much-needed campaign money for this Guyanese medical researcher, who lived on Long Island and did research in nephrology at my Alma Mater, the State University of New York at Stony Brook. I knew a few moneymen at the time, but they weren't biting on Guyana for some reason (lack of skill, no doubt).

I suppose I should mention here that from 1986 to about 1990 I was Vice President of the public relations company of John G. Gelinas & Associates on Fifth Avenue in New York. "Jack's" main, long-standing client was the country of Guyana, and had been for almost two decades. Weekly reports were sent directly to president Forbes Burnham in Guyana by diplomatic pouch. As it happens, one of my oldest friends is originally from Guyana. We went to CFS together.

Joe Armstrong, as some of us called him, went into the army and became a Major. His main area of expertise was The Patriot Missile, conveniently enough. It's funny how things work out, sometimes.

In West Virginia, where crime is almost non-existant (at least where I live), we have all kinds of gun lovers. In these "wild and wonderful" hills, you more or less have to own a gun, preferably one that will stop, or at least slow down, a bear if he's coming at you. Along with bears, rattlesnakes are about, and copperheads, too. There are critters and crawlers out here that you treat with respect, so much respect that when you encounter one you don't waste a lot of time finding that shotgun, or whatever. Rattlers need to be dispatched or they'll breed on your property somewhere. No thank you very much! My neighbor, a retired biochemistry professor, who is a little hard of hearing, didn't hear the rattlesnake at his door last summer. Fortunately for him someone else in the house did, and shot it on the spot. Poor thing.

So there is nothing really too unusual about a West Virginia man cleaning his 32-caliber, his 38-caliber, and 357-caliber pistols in the morning, or anytime. But what *was* a little strange, even out here, was that while cleaning his three guns he managed to shoot himself in the same foot with all three guns. Ouch!

Well, after the second or third reading, I noticed some very curious similarities between this story and the one above it, which also featured West Virginia prominently, since WVA is where the fireball was first seen not far from Green Bank Observatory, the birthplace of SETI. For one thing, there was the extraordinary *timing* of what one can be almost sure was *another* unprecedented occurrence. As we'll recall, the Peekskill meteor was the first ever both filmed and recovered. How many times in the 500 year history of guns has someone shot himself in either foot three times with three different pistols? I would wager zero times.

Then there was the fact that the man shot himself in the *right* foot three times -- not the left foot. This, of course, corresponded to the *right* signal-light being hit in Peekskill two days later.

Then there was the fact that the man shot himself in the right foot *three* times, not twice, not once, but *three times*! Is one really supposed to believe that these correspondences were coincidences? Sorry, not me, but then I'm an ETi-intoxicated man.

The reader is pardoned for thinking that I've really lost it here. Do I really believe these *self-inflicted* injuries had anything to do with extraterrestrials? Hey, sometimes I even ask myself this question. But, here again we have that certain signature -- a shooter *aiming* at and hitting a well-defined *target*. Of course, both events were alleged to be "accidents," but here the concept seems very much abused.

Here the number "3" appears with emphasis once again -- three guns and three shots. As we recall, this number figures rather prominently on the Chevrolet's license plate, the right side of the license plate, that is.

"Skill" doesn't begin to cover this one, I'm afraid.

There is another theory. It holds that the West Virginia man had no help whatsoever from ETi when he shot up his foot, that what occurred was due mainly to sheer drunkenness, and not much else. (Being drunk can do that to you.) The theory further contends that the ETi in residence at the time merely *noticed* the event in Princeton when it happened (as it notices absolutely everything else that goes on in our world), thought it quite emblematic of our species, and then proceeded to design the Peekskill and SL9 events. They put a whole lot of human data into a hopper, ran a few algorithms on it, and out popped the *meteoritic solution*.

The main problem with this theory is that Peekskill was tied to SL9's fragmentation in July 1992, not to the bullet impacts in Princeton. The numbers 933 on the license plate seem to confirm this, because SL9 broke apart on July 7, 91 days *before* Wednesday October 7, 1992. We'll recall that SL9 broke apart 93 days (3 months) before the Peekskill event.

Was there a "clue" to be found in the particular *town* in which the multiple shootings occurred? A reference to Albert Einstein seems plausible here. Einstein accepted a position as Professor of Theoretical Physics at Princeton University in 1933. The theory of general relativity is probably humankind's most profound single insight into the universe, not to mention a cornerstone of our current scientific worldview.

What can we make of the *state* in which the multiple shooting took place -- West Virginia? Well, this would be where the whole "Peekskill" thing started -- in the skies over West Virginia.

700 km flightpath of the Peekskill fireball. The long dashed line is based on a compilation of visual observations for the early part of the trajectory; the short dashed line is the theoretical (undocumented) initial portion of the trajectory.

Coincidence? Naa, which is to say, I doubt it strongly. It all ties together so well, after all. But, could the ETi responsible for Peekskill really be *that* good? Could they really induce a man to shoot his own right foot thrice? The attribution seems questionable, but seeing is believing. This aimer could probably hit a flea off a buck's antler from half a million miles out, if Peekskill is any indication.

Okay, sure, the man was a little drunk when he shot himself three times, which probably helped things along, but how does one *cause* a man to do this to himself? And, what could be the point of such a demonstration? A little reflection brings the clear and obvious answer. It was nothing less than a metaphor for the human condition. When you "shoot yourself in the foot" (hello!), you're acting like your own worst enemy. One can't blame Mr. Murphy, the vagaries of chance, or anything else, for we have no one to blame but ourselves for the predicament we find ourselves in. Now, when you shoot yourself in the foot *a few time*s, you're really not going anywhere, not very fast, anyway.

How did ETi accomplish this? I don't know, but then we're only a 200,000 year old intelligence, while ETi may be upwards of two *billion*. How much evolutionary time separates us from, say, the rhesus monkey? A few million years. You know what, maybe making a guy shoot his own right foot three times is not such a big deal, after all.

What I think ETi is telling us here by way of this event is that any nuclear wars that might come to fruition in the future simply *will not do*. Of course, that's just my opinion. Nonetheless, it is unsettling to think that extraterrestrials have this kind of control over human behavior. Attributing this kind of capability to this ETi makes it suddenly important for us to ascertain or feel for the "shooter's" *ethical constitution*. Before we attempt this, though, let's consider the case of the "government" shooter first. It is known that secret government research programs have perfected something somewhat akin to this capability. People can now become hypnotized or programmed to do things, terrible things, so that when a trigger word is uttered, the subject carries out missions they are not even aware of performing. The movie "The Bourne Identity" and its sequels starring Matt Damon was based on the MK-ULTRA/Monarch paradigm. Shoot ourselves in the foot?

Without going too far into this (because who wants to?), Monarch Programming is a method of mind control which relies on the victim's capacity to dissociate from reality, and permits the creation of walled-off personalities to hold and hide the cognitive programming. Used by numerous organizations for covert purposes, Monarch is allegedly a continuation of project MK-ULTRA, a mind-control program developed by the CIA, and tested on the military and civilians. The results can be horrifying: the creation of a mind-controlled slave who can be triggered at any time to perform any action required by a handler. Let's hope certain governments don't *cheat* with such a capability, now.

While all three events were very much keyed to the number 3, we now see the word "right" repeated. This seems to inform us of another *key* being used. The word "right" (as in, not wrong) conveniently carries connotations like morality, justice, precision (true and accurate), and truth. What's more, sentients have a choice between right or wrong. See how their plot thickens!

This apparent moral overlay exhorts the perceiver to re-touch, as it were, all the bases in the new light provided. We can conjure Columbus and NASA right off the bat, of course, but there are lots of other possible significant intersections, like "smart" missiles. I mean, how easy is it to push a button and wreak death and destruction three-hundred miles away? No pain and no painful images.

The "rightness" of this response to HRMS might just as easily be applied to targets three trillion miles away, as three-hundred, though. But, it's wrong. Even more important than this was the advanced notion that there *is* a right and wrong, which seems to be very trenchant news these days. Why *else* should ETi mention this dichotomy again if not to emphasize it?

"Every heart sings a song, incomplete, until another heart whispers back. Those who wish to sing always find a song. At the touch of a lover, everyone becomes a poet." -- Plato

Ten
How Intelligent?

"A wide range of extraterrestrial benevolence should be expected, considering the huge number of advanced civilizations thought to exist, the probable large differences in their forms and cultures, the hugely varying degrees of evolution which are implied, and the seemingly great difficulty or expense for any collection of such races to police the galaxy so as to stamp out any aggressive behavior noted."

J.W. Deardorff, Quarterly Journal of the Royal Astronomical Society, Dept. of Atmospheric Sciences, Oregon State University

Lurking beneath any assumptions about the aimers' benevolent intentions is a frightening theory with frightening evidence. I have never really considered the dispatchers of Peekskill and SL9 frightening, though, because I trust the correctness of my interpretation of the messages. I figure if the extraterrestrial(s) responsible for Peekskill and SL9 have evil designs on the human species, they would have probably executed those designs long ago. They would not have given us key information for our own long-term survival, nor given us so much to glean about their sense of fair play, their capabilities or personality.

On the other hand, I am sure there are any number of gloomy interpretations of these events possible. There may be whole aspects of the communication that I did not apprehend, specific signals and their implied meanings that I neglected to find. I guess the point is -- and it's an important point to make -- these signal-based communications can be interpreted in numerous ways by different people.

So I guess I would be remiss if I did not make mention of this, the other side of the double-edged sword, because a major part of this interworld exchange *was* its warnings. The main thing that gives me reason for some trepidation is what could happen to us if we should ignore these warnings, warnings like, "be careful what you *search* for."

Among the articles NASA-Ames sent to me in response to my apprising it of my ETi-meteor theory was one describing what the SETI community calls the "zoo hypothesis." It basically states that advanced extraterrestrials do not contact or intermingle with us in order to allow for our natural evolution and development. This hypothesis may not be far from the truth, but there now appears to be a bit more to it than this. If merely watching our behavior were to remain the full extent of their interest in us, they would not have given us such generous and informative clues about their existence and nature.

The question of whether Princeton/Peekskill/SL9 were meant to be a first testing step towards relations with our species remains to be seen. But what kind of relationship could this end up being? Would it be business as usual? Could this "business" ever be fair, or would the relationship eventually resemble that of Columbus and the technologically inferior natives he found? This subject needs an entire book, if several such books haven't already been written on this.

One thing appears certain, though. Technologically superior beings have so far refrained from greatly interfering with or exploiting our species. Their approach and attitude toward us remains "hands-off."

Perhaps this is ETi's general policy with respect to all galactically naive worlds known to them, or maybe the policy applies only to worlds exhibiting certain primitive characteristics. If the case happens to be the latter, then it could behoove us to improve our act considerably.

Considering the benefits that would come with membership in some galactic community, we could do well to effect a desirable change. As for the potential dangers inherent to such a course, I don't think the human race is one to shy away from the kind of opportunity that an intelligently inhabited galaxy might afford. So the issue of human fitness is an important one. Some say we are more "civilized" today than we were in Columbus's time. An objective accounting of this in terms of, say, "number of dead by war" could argue powerfully otherwise. Which is it? Well, I think one could safely say that post-modern man is a good deal more sanitary and healthy than his/her late antecedents from the middle ages. Beyond this, it may be difficult to discern a terribly large or meaningful difference.

The people who call the shots today are the ones the ETi would ostensibly have to deal with should they ever decide to make formal and full contact with us. What can be said about that group of a few dozen or hundred that actually make the world go round, the ones who fund and prosecute the wars, deliver and perpetuate the poverty, etc. Can this group be trusted? Are its methods and agendas ethical, peaceful, or salubrious for the species or the planet? Do its members act in a more civilized fashion than you or I? I don't think so, but that's just Tom six-pack talking. The fact is those who pull the strings today, as in centuries past, are not like you and me at all. At times, the strange code by which they live allows them, no, *encourages* them, to undertake things that you and I would consider beyond the pale of morality. They call it *realpolitik,* a term about which in candid moments they make no particular bones. But is this a sign of intelligence or one of tenaciously holding on to the reigns of power at any and all cost?

In order to answer, or at least throw light on this question, we could try and define the term "intelligence." I would identify five basic types or forms of intelligence: problem solving, social, secret, intuitive, and other. Each of these forms of intelligence performs a service for the species, including perpetuation of the species.

What kind of intelligence?

The first type would obviously be the ability to use logic to solve problems. This is the one that has allowed us to live a modern, technologically enhanced lifestyle, one that uses computers, airplanes, microwave ovens and automobiles. A species with no problem solving ability can survive in its habitat only so long as that habitat remains friendly toward it. Humans at present are able to survive most terrestrial situations, changes and calamities in some numbers but they are essentially unable to survive threats that occasionally originate from outside their natural environment. On this particular scale of intelligence, perhaps it might be said that we rate moderately high. (Of course, without too many tangible samples with which to compare ourselves, the conferment could be off somewhat.)

The second type of intelligence has to be social. This basically refers to the ability of a species to live together in peaceful cooperation. It determines how a species consisting of millions or billions of individuals manages to co-exist on a planet with finite resources and space. A socially unintelligent species may be able to survive in large numbers through sheer technological prowess but end up using that technology to periodically kill large swathes of its own population. (I believe we are one of those.) Such a species will not flourish because its groups spend too much of their time and resources killing each other rather than working out ways to extend the species, which in most cases means reaching out into space. Worlds in perpetual conflict will be unable to devote themselves to the quite considerable rigers of deep space, which cuts the species' chances to survive indefinitely down to few thousand years, or maybe just enough time for a large asteroid to come and end it all for them. Populous species may justify the mass killing of their own on the grounds that it makes the quality of life better for those who remain, but this is a sophistic and amoral excuse, especially when mass killing is conducted with the same frequency *before* the species becomes populous as after. Such a species will simply never stop the killing itself (and others).

Social intelligence is also the ability of a species to arrive at a set of firm principles concerning *right* and *wrong* and to stick by them. For example: Killing, slavery, injustice and deception are wrong. Life, freedom, justice, and truth are right. Some socially unintelligent species might hold these imperatives up as true and right but still be unable to hold to them in actual practice. The result of this is corruption, killing, stealing, injustice and slavery. These basic principles of conduct will be things that everyone *in the universe* can agree with. According to the philosophy of Kant, this seems as good a basis for a social philosophy or code as any. He writes, "Always act in such a way that the maxim determining your conduct might become a universal law; act so that you can will that everybody shall follow the principle of your action."

The third type of intelligence is that concerned with keeping information, agendas and knowledge secret. When secret agencies become corrupt, small unelected elites that rule by secrecy use this form of intelligence to increase and perpetuate their wealth, position and power. Secrecy becomes little more than a cover for corruption, allowing controlling elites to operate above the law. The "need to know" becomes a mechanism of compartmentalization so that crimes and agendas can be furthered at the highest levels with impunity, without the larger society, or even its paid funtionaries, knowing the larger picture. Without strict oversight, such agencies inevitably become rogue tools of the powerful, or even powers unto themselves.

I identify a fourth form of intelligence as stemming from unconscious and intuitive processes. It is a kind of *knowing* without necessarily knowing why. It is that reservoir of species knowledge composed of all our collective experience and knowledge. It can be as simple and visceral as knowing what the sharp snap of a branch in the jungle means to something as amorphous and nonvisceral as the television reporting that a meteor has just smashed through a car's signal-light. In both cases, a little intuition can be the best thing, for if we laugh off too many twig snaps or too many cosmic moos, calling them merely "subjective" or "anecdotal", then we can soon find ourselves in trouble up to our neck. Intuitive intelligence doesn't analyze the situation against complicated rules of evidence, it reacts. *It knows.* At the very least it suspects. It says, *something* is out there.

Intuitive intelligence is knowing the difference between coincidence and some significant Other(s) -- entities who at any time may decide to *create* instances of "happenstance" in order to relay a message while remaining anonymous. Reception is not a matter of faith here but rather one of sapient intelligence, intelligence in knowing when a large number of related "coincidences" accrue to something much more than just a multitude of separate coincidences.

Without our faculty of intuition, we wouldn't have stood a chance against predators going back hundreds of thousands of years. Intuitive intelligence is also that Knight-moving part of cognition that allows us to jump forward from what is already known. As we noted in chapter seven, without intuitive intelligence, science is useless, dead.

The fifth form of intelligence also resists being pinned down but might be renamed, *extra*-intelligence. I reserve it as a type unknown to us, a kind for which we may have few or only one example. It is simply something *else.* We assume its existence intuitively, from the highly probable fact that humans are not as intelligent as intelligent can get. An I.Q. of 10,000 may not be out of the question, should the measurement even apply.

How do humans weigh or rate on these intelligence scales? In most cases, not terribly well, I'm afraid. Human problem-solving appears to be one strength, though. On a scale of 1 to 100, perhaps we score a 70, but since intuitive processes are thrown to the back of the bus in our society, it may be closer to 50. For its part, secret intelligence is supposed to serve the national interest, but it rarely seems to do this anymore. Instead it appears to serve only self-serving foreign oligarchs, like the Federal Reserve, which means it serves the same interests that U.S. presidents have served since L. B. Johnson, or Truman, if you go back to "The System's" suspicious founding. As far as social intelligence is concerned, we would clearly score rather low. In the details infusing three unprecedented impact events we have before us, as big as night, an ETi who has given us the boon of a small peek at what "extra-intelligence" looks like. Their rather perfect performances credit us with the intelligence to discern them.

What I and possibly some others perceived that October night was a symbolic interworld communication dispatched by an advanced nonhuman entity, or entities. Implicit with this realization was the disconcerting understanding that our world has been monitored by extraterrestrials for years, or even centuries. They've been waiting for us! Now that we know this, the question becomes *now what?*

For now, this mystery will have to be added to that long list of deep mysteries concerning the *real* universe mentioned at the beginning of this book, mysteries that take in such things as black holes, dark matter, gravity, quantum mechanics, and membrane multiverses. The humbling fact is we really don't know what it's all about. The truly deep questions remain quite mysterious and dark. What we know or think we know pertains mainly to what we can see, but there is still *much* that we do not see. If extraterrestrials have solved and mastered *any* of these mysteries, many things might become possible for them, things which when employed here would seem quite magical or "impossible" to us humans.

Several scientists have argued the unlikelihood of any of this. Dr. Shostak at Ames Research Center (alias SETI Institute) seems to doubt that ETi could pull a thing like Peekskill off. In one letter he remarked that because the Peekskill meteor had no visible attachments for guiding the meteor to its precise target, the meteor could not have been aimed at anything. *"How do they 'fly' a meteor into a car? They would need sensors to be sure that the guy whose car was hit didn't stop at a gas station on the way, and park somewhere else. They would have to fly that rock down. Does that really make sense to you?"*

I suggested to this NASA spokesman that his was a slightly naive position to take, especially by someone in his position. *How* could they do it? Well, not with any human technology borrowed from our shelf, that's for sure. I tried to point out that our technology could be a rather puny thing compared to that probably millions of years in the making. I asked him to consider what a 16th century prelate would make of a human voice coming from a 20th century tape recorder? Some kind of evil spirit, no doubt, since no human would be seen to be visibly "attached" to the voice. I also pointed out that if they *had* attached some guidance system gadget to the meteor to guide it to its earthly target coordinates, this would have obviously spoiled the soup. It would have removed any uncertainty as to its intelligent causation *and* provided wreckage from which clues concerning their technology might be gleaned and reengineered. Surely, this could *never* do. But I might as well have been arguing the point with a 15th century priest. I even had to wonder whether or not the man was pulling my leg with the insipid denial routine.

Perhaps the feats performed were really not *too* many orders of magnitude more advanced than what The U.S. Department of Defense allowed to be displayed *ad nauseum* on television in 1990-1, when the first US/Iraq war was staged. These were the short videos showing America's latest toy, the Patriot missile. Although not quite as proficient in taking out Saddam's airborn SCUDS as first advertised (something like 60% were true to their mark), they did manage to intercept and prevent most of Saddam's SCUDS from reaching targets in Israel and Saudi Arabia.

ETi does not *ever* seem to miss what it aims at. No practice shots, beta-testing or trial runs were needed here. In fact, the marksmanship demonstrated was so hummingly precise, so dead on in other ways, that it is difficult to find fault or error of any kind in the shot.

The great fictional detective Sherlock Holmes once said, "Eliminate all other factors, and the one which remains must be the truth." While we can not completely rule out the theory that with no help from anyone and by complete blind coincidence, a 4 by 5 by 11-inch meteor plucked out a 4-1/2 by 22-inch target, leaving all the bordering chrome on two long sides intact, a serious detective would have to be stupid to completely ignore the mathematical probabilities involved. But then, science is not the work of detectives, is it? Science, for lack of a better word, is science, nothing more, nothing less. It has rules, and these rules are not to be broken, not by ETi, not by scientists looking for aliens, and most certainly not by yours truly. Somehow, I don't think ETi abides by too many of their rules.

I would even submit that the odds *against* blind nature doing what it did are a good deal larger than the odds of a technologically advanced extraterrestrial doing it. Although only a hunch on my part, I believe it is something Mr. Ockham of Occam's razor would approve of, especially if he were a proponent of the ubiquity of life theory. If the odds of intelligent life are anywhere near as high as Drake's equation predicts, then the probability of intelligent beings causing the Peekskill event seems at least as likely as the "random accident" theory, if not a good deal more so.

How do the odds for intelligent mediation improve if we throw in a little 20th century *relativity theory*? Einstein theorized that time slows down as a function of the velocity at which a physical body travels. This means that if one can achieve light velocity (C), time will essentially stop. But since by doing this a traveller would also acquire infinite mass, physicists tend to rule light-speed travel out. Okay, so what happens if a space traveller travels at 50% of the speed of light? Einstein tells us that the traveller would experience time much more slowly than a person on terra firma, so that when he returned to his planet of origin, more time would have elapsed on the planet than would have been biologically experienced by the traveller. With the slowing of biological time, a space traveller is able to span great distances of space with ease. If we then add something like suspended animation, a 500 or *10,000* year journey could seem quite short. Computers could navigate and run the ship while the crew mostly slept.

If we now consider the fact that all of our space-faring scenarios rely on a 20th century understanding of physics, it should be obvious that getting here from there is not really the problem. No, the problem now becomes how exactly to *approach* a world like ours. Should they bang us upside the head with news of their co-existence by landing on the White House lawn or dispatching a letter, in English, via radio-waves, or should they, in a different vein, blow softly at our ears? For any number of sound reasons they chose the latter approach.

Because their overtures helped commemorate and mark a quincentennial, the suggestion is made that communications from these intelligent beings occur only once every 500 years or so. Considering the questionable (and salient) history that distinguishes us on our world, this could be a bit more than we deserve, or maybe it is exactly what we deserve. Nonetheless, the fact that extraterrestrials are watching the goings on of our planet without directly interfering in them offers us encouragement, encouragement because it *was* the *right* signal-light that was pulverized, not the left; encouragement because they are clearly *not* the bloodless demons and destroyers of worlds that Hollywood so often likes to paint. Indeed, ETi was very explicit on this point. The Peekskill fireball was a *sporadic* meteor, not a Draconid; so ETi is not of a *draconian* bend *(whew!).* What's more, they do not apparently subscribe to the dour philosophies of Nietzche, Comte, Machiavelli, and Hobbes, who would probably find such kindly restraint a bit perplexing.

We see one maxim enacted in all of their signals: *wherever possible, do not interfere.* In our case, the axiom was only barely satisfied, because their actions did interfere with us; among other things, they changed our scientific opinion and attitudes toward a theory of geology known as *catastrophism*. But, notice they did *not* issue a warning, in English, or possibly French, saying something like:

"You vicious brutes make us ill. Why, wanton violence seems to be an everyday occurrence with you. You must follow our example of enlightened and constructive peacefulness ... or we'll give you a blast with a weapon so powerful you simply could not understand it."

or --

"Hi, we are the entities who watch. We come from a place where peace and tranquility reign and we shall use our superior brain to arbitrate your petty differences."

No, ETi's overture was not so conclusive or explicit as that. If it had been, how could a "relationship" be fair? It would have been a little bit like Europeans introducing themselves to the primitive peoples of the new world of Columbus's time (if we add a few million years and miles of difference). For all we know, the universe is not quite the peaceful place some of us like to think it is; maybe their lawful hint to us was meant to apprise us of this, in case we ever decide to send out any more "all points" bulletins. The next time we might not be so lucky-sevens and snake-eyes.

By leaving us alone and much to our own devices, ETi allowed us the *freedom* to decide what, if anything, to make of the signals and events in question. We were given the boon of a choice. How socially intelligent and ethical was that?

"It would be very nice if there were a God who created the world and was a benevolent Providence, ... a moral order in the universe and an after-life; but it is a very striking fact that all this is exactly as we are bound to wish it to be.." -- Sigmund Freud

Eleven
Those flying cars

UFOs are a subject with which I have had significant personal experience. I have authored several articles in such magazines and newsletters as "Saucer Smear", "UFO Universe", and "MUFON Journal." The first two publications were edited or published by old friends of mine in New York City. *"Smear"* is *still* going strong, well, going, after more than forty years now! These associations have given me ample opportunity to investigate both aliens and UFOs. I have attended my share of UFO symposia, conferences, and publicity stunts; I have even spoken at some of them. I know the game.

The trivialization of extraterrestrial existence by what amounts really to an extraordinary amount of hearsay, some of it incoherent or nonsensical, has not served to increase our knowldge or understanding of the issue, but rather to obfuscate it. How can so many sightings and claims of ET activity be reconciled with the paradoxical fact that no hard, universally acceptable evidence exists to support the postulation?

I was never particularly interested in UFOs, i.e. the cars, as I call them. Because my sub-interest in the field was always the aliens allegedly riding around *inside* the UFOs, I usually found myself pretty much alone among these peers. Harold, one of my closest friends back in the day, and I, used to argue for hours about the reality of UFOs.

A die-hard believer, Harold co-founded NICAP with Donald Kehoe in 1953 with the tidy nest egg his father gave him. Keyhoe was widely regarded as the leader in the field of ufology in the 1950s and early-to-mid 1960s.

I always thought the predilection of the UFO community for the technology over the flesh-and-blood entities a little irritating, and I never liked the cipher paper cut-outs that occasionally came out of it. The stick figures just never did it for me.

Toward the end of our long friendship, I had occasions to tell him about the Peekskill meteor event in terms of what it meant. If proof of the general indifference to nonhuman sentience were ever needed, then it came from this UFO enthusiast of fifty years, not to mention from a host of other heavy hitters in the field with whom I associated. Talk about irritating. Have you ever tried to reason with a hard core believer? Aliens have become so *hackneyed* it's not funny; it's most especially not funny for me.

As much as anything else, though, this experience has convinced me that I *must* be on to something, because I am sure the extraterrestrials do *not* appreciate the bloodless stereotypes the UFO field promotes. That is, if the intention of the designers was to control for anyone, the UFO posse would surely be right up there with SETI scientists.

Here in the form of eight common questions and their uncommon answers are my latest views on the subject.

Do you believe UFOs are real?

No, I am not a believer in UFOs, not as extraterrestrial spacecraft, anyway. On the other hand, yes, unidentified objects do exist in the air. Their frequency depends mostly on the training and sophistication of the observer, however. The more knowledge of aerial phenomena and flying machines the observer has, the more he or she will be able to accurately identify what is in the air.

My standards of evidence for the existence of extraterrestrials (not UFOs) are very high. I need something solid, something that *cannot* be faked. For me, Peekskill and SL-9 meet this standard.

UFOs, on the other hand, have been proven to have a large number of prosaic explanations. Finding these explanations is what serious researchers in the field spend a lot of their time doing. While a few cases remain unexplained and unsolved, this does not necessarily mean that extraterrestrials ride around in the ones that remain. The fact is mysterious phenomena still exist, but to attribute anything mysterious in the air to aliens is simplistic. That UFOs have become synonymous with alien spacecraft seems to be due to cultural conditioning or to some innate need to fill in that gaping blank on the puzzle board.

I find it difficult to reconcile how after thousands of UFO reports, not one shred of physical evidence from these sightings can be shown to anybody. Mr. Ockham would not approve. The small percentage of sightings that remain unexplained are probably due to a combination of human ignorance, very good trickery, or secret military activities. In the last of these bins, I would be willing to place a large number of unidentifiable sightings. Things that perform amazing tricks in the sky exhibit no purpose other than to wow an audience. I do not think advanced extraterrestrials are in the entertainment business, per se.

Honestly, I can't think of anything more idiotic than spindly grey men ("Greys") with huge black eyes -- paper cut-out humanoids, no less! -- riding around in UFOs abducting people from their sleep and performing genetic or other strange procedures on them. Nor do I really believe that *really advanced* extraterrestrials (the ones we are probably talking about) *need* UFOs or any other 20th century human notion of auto-transportation. Call it a hunch, but somehow I don't think they need such contraptions.

As for the famous Roswell case that started the whole business, it is likely the wreckage found strewn across a mile of New Mexico desert in 1947 was more or less what the Air Force eventually admitted it was -- a secret airborn spy balloon system (Project Mogul) used to listen for weak reverberations from nuclear test blasts originating in the Soviet Union. The explanation certainly seems logical.

In all my thirty years (1970 - 2000) of loose personal involvement with the alien posse, I have never encountered a UFO case that carried with it hard, museum-quality evidence of extraterrestrial activity. The *coup de main* of proof for the UFO enthusiast, the sheer volume of cases, thus seems to me to offer the best single reason to doubt their reality. The photographs and videos become less and less reliable for the simple reason that the technology of special effects (Fx) gets better and better, i.e. the saucers in the videos wobble less and less with every passing year. This is the sort of thing I tend to notice.

What's more, the military has had almost unlimited funding for decades now. One can be quite certain that every opportunity is being availed to invent or improve on technology that will make their hardware superior to that of their competition. Lights moving around in the sky? Sure. Wingless aircraft? Why not? They have the brains, they have the time, the facilities and the money. I mean, what more do they need?

Do you know of any UFO cases worth talking about?

Yes, but not because I see aliens riding in them, but rather because of the quality of the observations made. I was told by Martin Caidin, a knowledgable UFO source, sci-fi author and Air Force intelligence type that the majority of UFOs are natural phenomena. In an interview I did with him in 1988 for an astro-zine called "Thrust", Martin told me about a number of his encounters with UFOs. Here are two of them:

"I was flying with a guy named Keith Garrison out of New York. A bunch of us used to fly B-25 training flights in Florida. I wasn't in the military anymore by this time, but I'd go along with these guys and we used to fly the hell out of the things.

"We were in Northern Florida making a cross country flight diagonally across the state towards Patrick Air Force Base where we were going to land. Suddenly, one of the guys in the back of the airplane spotted a real bright light, well behind and above us, at about five o'clock on high. He said it looked as bright in daylight as you usually see Venus or Jupiter at night, which could have been a reflection from an airplane. Only this one kept getting closer and closer, so it obviously wasn't just a reflected light. He said the object looked like a disc. He called up front and said that this thing was catching up to us pretty fast, and descending, and is definitely a disc. Naturally, nobody had a hand-held camera. The only camera was in the bomb bays which were used for mapping.

"Well, this thing came up behind us and it was definitely a disc; it was perfectly round. We estimated, both from different positions from our aircraft and the shadows on the ground, that it was anwhere from a hundred to a hundred-and-fifty feet in diameter. If I remember correctly our own wingspan was about seventy-two feet. We dove down after it at full rpm.

"The disc kept descending until it fluctuated between 300 and 600 feet from the ground. There was the shadow of our B-25 on the ground and there was the shadow of the disc in front of us on the ground, as well. It reflected with the same kind of reflectivity as highly polished chrome or aluminum. It seemed to be sharp-edged, but 'sharp' could have been an illusion in this case. It showed no exhaust trail, no ports, no windows. It moved definitely under control. When it got in front of us, we pursued it. It always maintained about two-hundred yards in front of us, and for a while it went through some pretty wild maneuvers, banking sharply left and right.

"Our radioman was calling Patrick Air Force Base, and finally we got them on the radio. He told them what was going on and asked them to try and track us. But we were still too low. When we got close to the Ocala National Forest, it began to climb and we climbed up after it. Then Patrick picked us both up on radar. And then that sucker just accelerated and went up at about a forty-five degree angle away, according to radar, again between four and five thousand miles an hour. Gone. Off the scope."

This was an exceptional case, one of only a few UFO cases he or his "Bluebook" buddies couldn't explain. Generally, the situation went more like this:

"While we were screwing around and having a good time in the airplane, we got a call from Command at Otis saying, 'We have a report of an unidentified vehicle.' They gave us the headings and the altitude and that whatever this thing was it was being seen by hundreds of people, now by the thousands. It was being seen visually from the ground and visually air-to-air by pilots. It was being picked up on radar from the ground and on radar from the air. It was being reported to be moving at thousands of miles an hour with purple-blue flames out of one side of the disc and green flames coming out the other. Well, that's a pretty interesting one to go track down, so we vectored on a heading for it at full power.

"We started to climb and finally we saw it, and it was just the way they had described it -- all these tremendous flames coming out of it, and going at a tremendous rate of speed.The higher we climbed, the faster it was going. And, suddenly the object was in front of us at some unknown distance, and it was moving very slowly or not moving at all. Mac was saying, 'What the hell is this?' I said, 'Mac, take it back down two thousand feet, I've got an idea.' There was a very thin layer of cirrus below us and we went down just below it. The minute we were below that layer, the speed of the object picked up tremendously. So obviously we were getting a relative speed, like watching the moon through the branches of trees as you're driving along a road at night; the moon seems to be racing through the trees. It's really not racing at all, but you get that effect.

"I told Mac to take it back up again. When we broke above the cirrus layer, it stopped moving. We went down again and it speeded up. So what in the hell was this thing? I said, 'Mac, hang a ninety degree to the right. If this thing is what I think it is, we're seeing an ice crystal cloud, and refraction, the same effect as a prism with this ice. We turned the airplane to the right (we were cruising at about 500 mph), and just about five minutes later the lights dimmed out and there was a cloud.

"Then I said, 'Okay, buddy boy, let's reverse course and go the other way now.' When we got to the right sun angle, the thing exploded into colors again. Now ice crystals do reflect radar beams."

Here was a case where the UFO became an IFO under closer scrutiny. But, yes, there will *always* be things going on that defy explanation. The above is an excerpt from my interview of Martin Caidin published in the Winter 1990 (No. 35) issue of "Thrust" magazine -- science fiction and fantasy review.

Couldn't the Greys be responsible for Peekskill and SL9?

As far as I can make out, Greys are completely imaginary beings that exhibit all the cliched earmarks of a myth. Myths are a kind of collective hallucination.

I see no similarity between the mawkish, bug-eyed ciphers that masquerade in the public imagination as aliens, on the one hand, and the creators of the Peekskill, Princeton, and Shoemaker-Levy events, on the other. If one puts Peekskill/Shoemaker next to any other UFO case, no similarity in style or substance appears. Besides, UFO aliens have nothing to say and never have. The ETi responsible for Peekskill on the other hand is fairly bursting with purpose and self-expression. ETi presents ironies, performs cultural tests, and even seems proud of their skill. They propound in a multi-eloquent way on moral issues. In short, ETi exhibits a *personality*.

Why would aliens use meteors and not radiowaves to communicate?

Given the less than significant result of Peekskill and Shoemaker-Levy 9 in terms of our actually receiving a message, the events in question may have been intended more as a beta-test or probe of human receptivity, historical conscience, and thinking patterns, to posit a few.

If it's possible to imagine American indians asking the same question, it might be rephrased like this: why didn't ETi use smoke signals to transmit their message? The answer in both cases would be that this advanced ETi just doesn't use such archaic methods to transmit messages. For that matter, maybe it never did.

Seriously, though, why move precipitously and irreversibly when a gentle nudge might be more appropriate, more heuristic? Why, there must be *many* interesting and gainful ways to broach contact with another world besides that of *radio-waves*.

The people who fund the radio-telescopes and run this planet are not the sort they would probably want to have much to do with, anyway. They are too often devious, unprincipled, ruthless liars who cannot be trusted for a moment. They wage war constantly. They are forever on the lookout for ways to consolidate and increase their power and don't really care what they have to do to accomplish this. As for the scientists who man their facilities, they wouldn't know an intelligent signal if it fell on them. (This was ETi's joke, not mine.)

Aside from this, extraterrestrials can be expected to have their *own* agendas, methods, and protocols, especially as these relate to the touchy business of making contact with a primitive, planet-bound species like ours. They will have a codex or policy borne of long experience to guide them. Hey, *worlds* are involved here.

As mentioned previously, pragmatically speaking, meteors gave ETi plausible deniability. They were able to do two things simultaneously:

1) transmit vital information to us, such as informing us that comets do impact planets and 2) *broach* contact with our world without disclosing any strategic or vital information about themselves. What's the hurry?

Despite a large amount of circumstantial evidence, there is really nothing that we can actually use or exploit from the events. The messy, unpredictable, and probably undesirable effects of changing our world and worldview overnight was artfully finessed, and with good reason.

ETi's hands-off appoach allowed them to tweak and ping humanity, or perhaps more specifically, human scientists. One specific area of interest in the latter case would have been to gauge the strength of scientific intellectual attachments. How tenaciously do these "probers" of the galaxy hold to their rigid and often narrow preconceptions and methodologies?

Another reason an ETi might avoid using radio-waves concerns the fact that governments receiving the radiowave signals can be expected to keep any such findings secret. The hope of gaining some future advantage over competing nations would be too strong to resist. A government would only need to evoke the "National Security" and whatever finding was made could be snatched from the public domain and stamped "secret." I myself kept the historic intelligence secret, until such time as I could find a decent publisher for the story (I never did). Who wants to be second when reporting such news?

Unless the ETi's objective was to make secret contact with a particular intelligence agency, this likely eventuality could not have been very useful or satisfactory from an extraterrestrial's perspective. On the other hand, the signals they did send were made available to everyone on the planet.

Are aliens colluding with super-secret military cabals? And, what about the recovered (mostly dead) aliens residing in secret Pentagon laboratories?

Another fine myth, if you ask me. In my time as a UFO insider I have seen and heard a lot of claims about secret cabals colluding with aliens. Aside from the fact that proof for these claims is nonexistent, the notion does not really bear logic. A little common sense applies. Does anyone really think that extra-terrestrials would be stupid enough to allow humans to capture and study one of their ships and its occupants, dead or alive? How intelligent would that be?

If we assume for the moment that aliens actually use UFOs to get around, then, if an accident or system error befell one of these ships (a potential and inevitable occurrence), wouldn't the ETi think to deploy a self-destruct mechanism to prevent humans from data-mining their technology *and* DNA? I simply cannot imagine any alien overlooking such a crucial contingency. But, if we were to assume that aliens -- some alive and some dead -- are being disected or tortured for information in secret laboratories, how would this endear us to them to the point that they would willingly collude with our military on secret moon bases? *Please.*

I have personally heard it disclosed in a "closed-door" United Nations briefing that a secret moon base exists that is co-operated by aliens and some "above-top-secret" military elite. Although I do not recall the speaker's name (I place the meeting somewhere in the mid-1980s), I do recall that he was Belgian and well respected in the UFO field for his books and articles. The slide-show-assisted presentation was delivered to an interdisciplinary group (club) of about fifteen. It was not convincing in any provable sense. It may have *sounded* good to the U.N. audience, and my two colleagues, but not to me. According to our U.N. sponsor (the same one I had been in touch with on the WRAP system), we three interlopers were not supposed to be able to listen to the presentation, but if this were really the case we wouldn't have been there at all. We were immediately detained and questioned by U.N. security after the meeting. It must have been pretty obvious who had let us slip into the meeting that afternoon because one of us was a U.N. official, so we were let go. The "closed door" designation probably had more to do with the rather bizarre and potentially embarrassing nature of the presentation (for the group's members) than to any secret information being disclosed.

By no real evidence, I mean nothing was proven, only described in great detail and with lavish color drawings. No photographs of the base were presented, of course. As something of an expert even then, I knew the signs. I had heard it all a dozen times before, and I told our sponsor so. Of course, I couldn't disprove anything the Belgian said either, but that's the nature and lure of UFOs.

If secret military cabals exist on U.S. soil without being accountable to either the American people or their government, they are rogue and should be considered *highly* dangerous. It must be assumed that whatever they are up to, it is not to benefit anyone but themselves, or whoever funds them.

If aliens exist as you say, then doesn't this necessarily also mean that alien spacecraft (UFOs) exist? How else could they get here?

Not at all, and let us try and count the ways. A conscious entity whose provenance extends up to two-and-a-half billion years will not ride around in UFOs. I can't prove this, I just know it. As to how they get here, I would think that entities like these would have figured out quite a few things by now that enable them to get around or to see what's going on here without the use of space cars or any other faulty contraption.

What about all the officials and ex-military brass now breaking secret protocols to testify about alien spacecraft. What about all the ancient and not so ancient art which depicts aliens?

I don't believe any of this qualifies as convincing evidence of alien activity or existence. Like anyone else, 'officials' and even 'experts' are susceptible to the consensual hallucination that are UFOs. Some may have been paid to lie, although I shouldn't doubt that others are not lying, but are caught up in the attention they receive. For the most part, these "whistleblowers" are preaching to the UFO choir, telling them all exactly what they want to hear.

Zecharia Sitchin's work is uncorroborated by other scholars, so we have to take his word for everything, which I don't. He's made too much money telling certain markets what they want to hear (or read) for me to take him too seriously. I see his Anunaki story as myth, and he himself as a myth maker, nothing more. Also, I have attended some of his talks. My eyes, ears and gut tell me he is laughing all the way to the bank. Call it body language.

The often-cited ancient religious drawings and sculptures depicting "previous alien visitations" have alternate explanations. Many were the ritual masks and whimsical costumes of our ancestors. It is not hard to imagine that a good many of the artful and wildly imaginative costumes of our ritual-happy ancestors would resemble beings not quite of this world. Gods, demons, spirits, and animal composites might easily remind us today of how aliens might look. It seems to me that Van Daniken and others have made rather cavalier use of these and many other "appearances", so much so that I do not waste a lot of time tracking down very many of these claims.

Considering the potential for UFOs to be used by powerful special interests to gain psychological control of populations by manufacturing false alien events, and considering the secret technologies now available to some of these players, I wouldn't believe any offi cial or unofficial "disclosure" on the subject of aliens that did not meet the basic standard that Peekskill and Shoemaker-Levy present.

"There is something in the unselfish and self-sacrificing love of a brute, which goes directly to the heart of him who has had frequent occasion to test the paltry friendship and gossamer fidelity of mere Man." - Edgar Allan Poe

Twelve
Like a rock!

Remember those Chevrolet commercials run during the mid to late nineties showing this or that Chevrolet truck scrambling up and over steep hills and rugged boulders? Remember the pitched refrain, *"Like a rock!"*? I wonder if Chevrolet's advertising agency caught wind of my theory regarding Peekskill. And, speaking of Chevrolet, is it possible to think of a better choice for a brand of car than the one that so succinctly captured, in graphic terms, exactly what befell that parked Chevrolet in Peekskill?

My publisher informs me that I am not allowed to reproduce the Chevrolet logo in the pages of this book due to copywrite infringement law. At the risk of asking you, dear reader, to commit a thought crime, let me ask you to view the graphic below. Now picture in your mind the actual Chevrolet logo, which is not very different from the graphic. Obviously, ETi's choice of a Chevrolet was spot on, like virtually everything else about the Peekskill event. In a word, the logo said it all.

Okay, somehow ETi's target car *had* to be a Chevrolet. What else would ETi choose, a Subaru, Dodge, Mercedes, Pontiac, Nissan, or Bentley? Now, the name Chevro-*let* did ping your humble driver. I mean, what is a hackney if not something to let? (Sorry, just dreaming.) No, ETi's choice was dead-on. The trick was in finding a Chevrolet in Peekskill, for the town clearly *had* to be Peekskill, with an owner whose 18th or 21st birthday was October 12, *and* whose license plate could convey the many dates and other meanings desired. But in order for ETi to find this perfect target among all the other targets in the United States, it would need to know a lot about this country. At the very least, ETi would have had to know what was written on every license plate in Peekskill, the exact location of every car, what everybody's birthday was (tricky), and, of course, what every town in the country is called. ETi would also have needed to know that the capital of the United States is Washington, D.C., where the National Radio and Astronomy Observatory is located, and, of course, the significance of the appellation, *Draco the Dragon*. If the impacting meteor had been a Draconid meteor instead of a sporadic meteor, we might well have inferred that someone of a *draconian* nature had suddenly come our way. Fortunately for us, this would never do.

One does get the feeling from this that there is not very much going on in this world that ETi doesn't know about, or have access to. This might come as unsettling news to certain government agencies that like to keep secrets. And, if these agencies think they can out-crypto ETi, they should try and even imagine what ETi's math is like.

Another rather haunting ETi capability is suggested by the *threshold* level result of their overture. They would have to be sure that at least *someone* in the country (or world) picked up on their signals. One person would need to be there to perceive the tree (meteor) falling in the forest. Otherwise, what would be the point? It made *my* day, I can tell you, and that's all I'm going to say on this.

Some background

As a professional publicist for a number of years, I thought I knew why the media was suddenly ignoring everything of mine of any importance. My subject was too scientific, too new or too old, too controversial -- too something, yet I always suspected that this might not be the underlying reason. I am the hack who hacks, right through the bull. This is what I do, but the mass media doesn't do or appreciate that. Still, I have always made this priority one.

I don't recall exactly when it was that I first suspected something was going on beneath the veil of reality, the reality promulgated in school, books, magazines, the movies and televised media, but it must have been during my freshman or sophomore year of high school. While many of the kids of my generation were rebelling against hair regulations (the cool ones wore wigs over their long hair), dress regulations or the Vietnam war, I was rebelling against the entire consensus reality. I was the one who doubted very much what he was being taught in history class. I remember the subtle messages underlying our class discussions concerning the roots of our western culture, as well as those of the school's principle concerning my future history, should I continue the way I was going. Society in general doesn*t* reward this sort of thing. I don't suppose it ever has. As a result, it has not really been made possible for me to make much of a living at what I do, editorially speaking, though still I do it. Someone has to.

In addition to the case presented in this book, let me provide a few examples of what I mean about "underlying historical realities" that have come to my attention over the years.

I was the first to apprise the media of my friend and client, Martin Caidin's passing, from cancer in Florida, on March 24, 1997. Martin was a very important writer and historian. He was the author of at least eighty fiction and nonfiction books, one of which (Cyborg) led to the popular 1970s television series, "The Six Million Dollar Man." Another became the 1969 science fiction movie, "Marooned," starring Gregory Peck and David Janssen. The media ignored my press release and Martin's passing even though Martin Caidin was one of the most influential writers of the 20th century. He also wrote hundreds of screenplays (I know).

Aside from being an author on aeronautical history, science fiction, military science, and para-science, Martin was the co-founder of the American Astronautical Society, advisor to presidents, a NASA broadcaster, lecturer, documentarian and TV producer. Caidin was also singularly instrumental in bringing about a thaw in east-west (Soviet/U.S.) relations.

According to an official NASA report and a letter penned by Phillip Handler, former president of the National Academy of Sciences, the movie "Marooned" was directly responsible for the 1975 joint US-Soviet space mission known as Apollo-Soyuz. In a head-to-head meeting with his Soviet counterpart, Dr. Mstislav Keldysh, head of the Soviet Academy of Science, Handler suggested that it would be nice if the United States and Soviet Union could work together on a mutual space program or mission like in the movie, "Marooned." Keldysh scoffed at the idea, but asked Handler what movie he was talking about. Handler then told him about Martin Caidin's movie about American astronauts marooned in space unable to return to Earth. He related how a team of Soviet cosmonauts come to the Americans' rescue in space and save the astronauts lives. This so impressed Keldysh that he responded "You are the first American I have ever met without horns."

Years earlier Martin Caidin had co-authored the biography I Am Eagle (Indianapolis, Bobbs-Merrill), with Soviet cosmonaut Gherman Stepanovich Titov. This 1962 book was a celebration of this cosmonaut's life, the second man in space, the first man in space being Yuri Gagarin. The book contained information and never before seen photographs of the Soviet space program. Before the publishing of I Am Eagle, details of the Soviets' space program were a complete mystery to American analysts. Martin's co-authorship with the high level conrad, coupled with his subsequent movie, "Marooned", were major blows that broke the ice between the super-powers and paved the way for the joint space mission to take place.

On May 18, 1988 it was General Gherman Stepanovich Titov who greeted Western reporters at the super-secret Cosmodrome, which he headed, and where 289 Soviet launches had taken place. It was this unprecedented and publicized opening to the West, along with the first-ever publishing in the U.S.S.R. of A. Rybakov's docu-novel <u>Children of the Arbat</u> (1988) that signaled an end to the cold war. The peoples of the U.S.S.R. and the West were then experiencing *perestroika* (restructuring) and *glastnost* (openess). The book, which contained the truth about the monster, Stalin, woven into its story, changed the entire psychology of Russia, and led to its peaceful unfettering by late 1990.

I had been informed of Marty's death by his wife, Dee Dee, the day after it happened. I sent out press releases to this effect but received no response. But then, by this time the media had been given reason to be truly sick of hearing from me. I had become a persona non grata. You see, by October 1992, the media had received an earful from me on Krebiozen. Remember that one? In fact, Krebiozen was about all I had been working on when "Peekskill" went down. Consequently, any and all news from me on the Peekskill event will have been taken as pretty good, if not glad, evidence that I had fallen off the deep end, and should therefore be even more assiduously ignored, if this was possible.

By the way, the reason I got to know Martin Caidin was because his 1988 book, <u>Exit Earth</u>, put me in rivets. It was the most stunning piece of science fiction I think I have ever read, and I've read a *lot* of science fiction over the years. In fact, at the time I was science fiction editor of "Rave Reviews" magazine. After reading this 800-page novel for review, I simply had to go down to Gainesville and interview this man. The book is about a *comet* that threatens to destroy the world, but mostly about the fast-tracked building of a space ark to take at least some remnant of humanity out of harm's way, and to the stars. If there was a point to the book (Marty didn't believe in "messages" in his books), I believe it was this: *We could do it.*

In case the reader is wondering what he thought about Peekskill *et al*, he was of the "meteors hit the earth all the time" school. Unfortunately, I was never able sit him down long enough to explain it all to him. Needless to say, exposition of this material may not be easily reducible to news sound-bytes.

The WRAP solution

Way back in 1983 I had another occasion to fail in my public relations efforts. There was this new refinement of a 30-year-old concept called The Water Reclamation - Algae Production Process. As developed by ERA Associates of Lubbock, Texas in 1981, this WRAP system had far-reaching potential in fighting water-born diseases and starvation in the Third World, not to mention its efficacy elsewhere. Up to sixty (60) tons of protein-enhanced algae-cake per acre per year was being produced with the sewage processing system, a system that also produced industrial-quality water as an effluent. Sixty tons per acre compares with one or two tons per acre for conventional food crops. The algae-cake produced by the system was suitable for livestock feed. With modifications on flavor and consistency, the algae might even be made palatable; with a final polish, the effluent water could be made potable.

About 30 million people, mostly children, die every year in places like Africa due to bad water caused by untreated sewage and lack of food. A little applied common sense could easily end a lot of this, or so I imagined. Despite my repeated and prolonged efforts to bring this technology to some sort of public awareness, the media never showed the slightest interest in the technology.

When I was messing around the United Nations in the early eighties, I obtained a press release from the office of FAO Director-General Edouard Saouma calling for "renewed efforts to achieve global food security" on the basis of a report he prepared for the FAO committee on World Food Security. Mr. Saouma cited among the "catalogue of paradoxes presented by the world economic scene" the fact that global expenditures were standing at 20 times the total of overseas development assistance. Toward the end of the second page of this press release was the following morbid statement.

"Forty million people -- half of whom are children -- die every year from hunger and malnutrition. It has been said that if we were to observe a minute's silence for evey person who died in 1982 due to hunger-related causes, we would still be standing in silence all throughout this century and beyond."

I learned about the WRAP process from my best friend at the time, the husband of my former girlfriend who consulted for the company that developed the process. Michael Aitken was, among other things, an algologist who enhanced the system's algae product with higher qualities of protein. Michael Aitken was something of a genius, and rich, too, but not because he married into the Hartford A&P family. Michael was adopted by a very wealthy family. He built his first laser at the age of 15, his first plasma-jet at 17. At 18 he was teaching his Tesla-based, bone-mending techniques in mid-western medical schools. Although he never earned a PhD or M.D., Buckminster Fuller once introduced him to a symposium as "The Great Dr. Aitken." You see, Michael was miles ahead of the academic pack. Unfortunately for science, Michael died of a rare blood disease while in his mid-thirties *(damn!)*.

If on the other hand the subject of my press release or news happened to be relatively unimportant, that is, if my client happened to be a painter, a friend of the Pope, a world renowned flamenco dancer, a best-selling author, or a politican, the media had no problem. But if the subject was Krebiozen, hunger or Extraterrestrials, well, you know what I could do with it. Such things were just too big, too controversial, or too new to credit. In the case of Krebiozen, "official medicine" would not want the history of Krebiozen spread about in the news. And, what possible excuse could there be for shelving (to put it mildly) nature's very own non-toxic, immunological, cell growth regulator, not to mention a damn fine treatment for Cancer? Well, that's unmentionable (alas!)

The underlying significance of the Princeton/Peekskill/SL9 events lies in their ability to warrant and hold mankind accountable for his global condition. The world is sick, starving, corrupt, and largely dysfunctional, *by design,* not through blind forces that operate beyond comprehension or control. This, anyway, is how another intelligent race must surely see our planet. One cringes to think how little they miss of what goes on here.

That extraterrestrials would deign to even talk to us is proof that we own the intellectual tools to effect our own salvation, because if we didn't, why would they bother? If the profiteers of war would direct their time and energy into space rather than on seizing everything worth seizing through spec wars and propaganda, our species could develop habitats on the near planets or their moons. It is imperative that humans do this because major disasters can and will happen. Scientists tell us it is only a matter of time before the sun hiccups or sneezes, or an asteroid takes revenge on a bio-galactically deficient species like ours. And, if it's worlds that they want, then what better way could there be to obtain one than to stake out a nice fresh planet somewhere and call it their own?

Not like a rock, exactly, but mighty curious

Did the events of 933 augur the events of 911? The allusion is hard to miss, so too are their many corollaries. What may be harder to miss is that "9/11" was *not* planned and executed by a guy in a cave, or that buildings one, two *and* seven of the World Trade Center did *not* pancake because buildings one and two had airplanes crashed into them. Almost any engineer or architect can tell you that jet fuel fires simply can not melt structural steel. The media does not report this, or a hundred other things, because the media reports what it is told to report, and nothing else (it's why they're paid the big money); which is to say, investigative reporting does not exist within their ranks anymore (just ask Julian Assange or Alex Jones).

Now, there were some very curious similarities between the events of 911 and 933. Both event-sequences had official explanations that were untrue. Both had truer explanations that the average layman, in the former case, and SETI scientists, in the latter case, did not under any circumstances *want* to believe. There is the common idea of "guided missiles" (planes, meteors) being aimed at and hitting specific targets. There is the idea of history changing by and pivoting on both these events.

As with the three impactful events of 911, the number three (3) was also used as a signature for the creators of the events of 933. In 2001, if we still remember, much was made of the fact that there were three *coordinated* attacks. In the 933 *trio* of events there were *three* coordinated signals or impact events, *three* gunshots from *three* different guns, and *three* days separating Peekskill from HRMS activation. We are shown an isosceles *triangle*. We are even given the square and cube of 3 -- i.e. **9** October, and **27.3** pounds.

Did ETi see every phase and detail of 911's planning and execution, the most brazen, dastardly, and significant political crime of the century? Of course they did! That would be why they signed their little interworld communique, "933." Can there be any real doubt that 933 was meant to point up, even highlight, the events of 911?

But wait a minute, how can this be? 933 happened nine years *before* 911. Generally, things that happen nine years in the future can *not* be known with certainty and specificity in the present. This is a big problem, but maybe it's not so big a problem for Peekskill and SL9's creators. Can we at this point comfortably chalk off "933's" allusions to "911" as mere coincidence? Hey, it's possible that a *real* coincidence snuck in here; it happens. But I'm not buying it, not for a minute!

Don't ask me to explain how it could be done. My guess is ETi has plumbed *all* the way down the rabbit-hole, past worm holes, Higgs bosons and quantum gravity, maybe even past what we comfortably think of as cause and effect. I would point out, again, that these are *advanced* entities.

Time travel? Well, what happened nine years before 911 may be evidence as good as any that the theories regarding backward time travel are *indeed* possible; we already know, or think we know, that forward time travel is possible simply by achieving relativistic velocities (see chapter 10), even if not so simple to do. But this show behind the show, this invisible dog whose tail we saw wagging from October '92 to July '94, puts things on a whole other level, a level on which gods, not dogs, reside.

Timeslips like these don't just happen. There is a reason, a pattern, behind their occurring. Those who have learned to control them do so with impunity and anonymity, but not necessarily with personal profit or avarice in mind. It is our job as percipients of this particular timeslip to afford one last benefit of a doubt, and take its meaning to heart, to even divine a grand purpose. We are more than intelligent enough to do this, and maybe it was partly for this reason that we were given a *peek* at one, just this once.

If we accept that coincidence had nothing to do with these events, then time travel is not just a theory, it is historical fact. So the question becomes, why show us this? Maybe we are shown this because we are learning enough now in our current stage of technological development to be dangerous, not just to ourselves, but to Others. Maybe now we *need* predicting (i.e. futuristic oversight, or policing) and ETi was letting certain global elites know this.

As for the events of "911" and other similar pages of our recent history, it seems from sources in the independent media that most of the history-changing events that dot our history are *not* controlled by "blind forces that operate beyond comprehension or control", but rather by powerful and secretive forces for the purpose of spinning them in the news. One only has to use his eyes and brain to figure that one out.

Surely, there is more for the common man to hope for than war, mayhem, starvation, and despair, this never-ending cycle of building up and tearing down. There is! Call it what you want, but a new chapter and epoch of human history has already begun. Based on principles handed down by the Age of Enlightenment, mankind now seems poised to give individual freedom and dignity another run. As the light of day burns its way through the fog of lies and misconceptions accreted over generations, millions are beginning to once again use their eyes and brain to see what is being done to them, and to the world, by not so well-meaning elites.

Humans have unbelievable potential and unbounded talent. There is incredible beauty in the mind of (wo)man. But we are squandering this talent in unfruitful and destructive ways. Let us rediscover our heritage so that we can live in peace and prosperity and decency. Imagine what the world *could* be, with a little help from our friends.

And therefore as a stranger give it welcome. There are more things in heaven and earth, Horatio, Than are dreamt of in your philosophy. William Shakespeare, "Hamlet"

Thirteen
Will ETi call U.N.?

In November 1999, Kofi Annan, then Secretary-General of the United Nations, appointed an obscure Malaysian astronomer, Dr. Mazlan Othman, to be Director of the United Nations Office for Outer Space Affairs (UNOOSA) in Vienna. Eleven years later, several news sources reported the United Nations would soon appoint Dr. Mazlan Othman to be the official U.N. Ambassador for extraterrestrials. The claim turned out to be bogus and the appointment was never made, but the non-appointment was able to garner worldwide media attention to the tacit proposition that the U.N. might be the global agency best suited for the role of greeting and interfacing with extraterrestrials, should this ever occur.

The issue of whether the United Nations is the appropriate human agency to respond to communications from extraterrestrials might be resolved were it to officially acknowledge the signals already sent. This seems highly unlikely. The United Nations is not an organization to go out on a limb, or to be the first to accede to a theory that science has so roundly snubbed.

In a 2011 paper entitled, "Supra-Earth affairs", Dr. Othman wrote:

"Rapid developments in the detection of extra-solar planets augur well for those hoping to detect planets that would provide the right ecosystems for life...The continued search for extra-terrestrial communication, by several

entities, sustains the hope that someday humankind will receive signals from extra-terrestrials."

If it seems ironic that "someday" arrived shortly before NASA commenced the High Resolution Microwave Survey. There is even stranger irony in the fact that the U.N. will be unable to publically acknowledge or make use of ETi's floated communications, even if it wanted to. I think this was intentional on ETi's part, but who knows? It seems clear, however, that the two parties are not operating on the same wavelength. The only opening between the parties appears to lie in bridging the divide between the social and linguistic sciences and the so-called hard sciences in terms of their differing standards of proof. The signals presented in this book could be a good starting place for any enhancement or refinements in ETi receptivity that might be made.

Since your author is the first human *individual* to perceive, document and reveal an ETi communication, a choice may have already been made in this regard. If ETi did somehow choose its perceiver (yours truly), I'm not surprised, because I have been not only willing but keen to entertain an extraterrestrial's point of view. This, alas, is really all that's needed in order to perceive these events. It is also what will prevent UNOOSA from acknowledging ETi's overture, which in my way of thinking more or less disqualifies the organization for the role it seeks. Denial of these brilliantly timed and executed signals can only communicate a closed and negative regard for *any* nonhumans not willing to conform to human expectations.

Some history

From as early as 1977, the United Nations Committee on the Peaceful Uses of Outer Space (COPUOS) has raised the question of extra-terrestrial civilizations. In parallel with these developments, a message was put aboard two Voyager spacecraft launched in August and September of 1977. The following message was inscribed within a work of fine art and sent to the edges of the solar system.

As the Secretary-General of the United Nations, an Organization of 147 Member States who represent almost all of the human inhabitants of the planet Earth, I send greetings on behalf of the people of our planet. We step out of our Solar System into the universe seeking only peace and friendship; to teach if we are called upon; to be taught if we are fortunate. We know full well that our planet and all its inhabitants are but a small part of this immense universe that surrounds us, and it is with humility and hope that we take this step.

This was the United Nations' first message to any extraterrestrials "out there." Highly interesting is what could have been ETi's salient reply to this greeting. I refer, of course, to the one delivered in Peekskill, New York, on the night of October 9, 1992. That erstwhile reply highlighted and questioned the words "We step out … seeking only peace and friendship," with the following question: *"Do you mean like Christopher Columbus and those who followed him to the last 'new world' did?"*

UNOOSA eventually prepared a report, entitled "Messages to extraterrestrial civilizations." Following a debate on the details of this report, COPUOS posed the following question: should a register of messages to extra-terrestrial civilizations be established and maintained? One could propose instead that a register be started of messages *from* extraterrestrials.

At its third Conference on the Exploration and Peaceful Uses of Outer Space (UNISPACE III) in 1999, the topic of Near Earth Objects(NEOs) was taken up by several member states. Their concern over the threats of NEOs to the Earth and humanity was expressed in the Action Plan of the UNISPACE III Vienna declaration:

Action should be taken to improve the international coordination of activities related to near-Earth objects, harmonizing the worldwide efforts directed at identification, follow-up observation and orbit prediction, while at the same time giving consideration to developing a common strategy that would include future activities related to near-Earth objects.

Soon thereafter, Action Team 14 was created, which was chaired by the United Kingdom. This Action Team later brought the subject matter to the Working Group of the Scientific and Technical Subcommittee of COPUOS in 2004. In 2006, a Working Group was formed, which was again chaired by the United Kingdom. In its report in 2009, the Scientific and Technical Subcommittee determined that early detection and precision tracking were the most effective tools for the management of threats posed by near-Earth objects. Mention was also made of the international teams in various countries that were currently searching for and cataloguing near-Earth objects, including the Association of Space Explorers (ASE).

In a Draft recommendation for international response to the near-Earth object impact threat, UNISPACE III put out the following statement:

"Since there is a real possibility that mitigating measures, such as deflection, could be used and because the process of deflection intrinsically results in a potential but temporary increase of risk to populations not otherwise at risk in the process of eliminating the risk to all, the United Nations would be the most appropriate body to call on to facilitate the global effort to evaluate trade-offs and arrive at decisions on what actions to implement collectively."

Trade-offs? What in the world does *this* mean? By what logic would these decisions be made, or, more precisely, by *whose* logic would they be made? Inquiring minds want to know. That the U.N could even entertain such decisions strikes me as monstrous, though I suppose they are all in a day's work for an organization with ambitions and opinions of itself as high as those of the United Nations.

If we were to wake up one morning with the news that a large asteroid or comet was bearing down on Earth, there can be no discussion of who "gets it" and who doesn't, only that of how to take the bogey completely out of our way. The very idea that one could control or direct the damage that such a cosmic body would bring is not only absurd and psychically unhealthy but extremely unbecoming. Whether the U.N. wants to admit or not, it has an extra-solar *public* now.

"When we do (make contact), we should have in place a coordinated response that takes into account all the sensitivities related to the subject. The United Nations forums are a ready-made mechanism for such coordination. To make this happen, the champions of this subject must engage a wider audience, especially Member States of COPUOS, which would allow the subject to be included in the agenda of COPUOS and from this platform take it further to the General Assembly. The path through which the NEO issue was navigated is one that could provide a suitable example for the strategy and action to be taken by Member States."

I have endeavored herewith to engage "a wider audience", though I don't suppose Dr. Othman had someone like me (some guy) in mind when she invoked the notion.

COPUOS was set up by the U.N.'s General Assembly in 1959 basically to review, promote and discuss peaceful uses of outer space. But the phrase "peaceful uses" comes off a bit hollow. Question: What are the deeds of the United Nations on the planet world called Earth? People still starve to death in Africa at the rate of thirty million a year. Deaths due to poor or no sanitation and disease remain at appaulling levels. Aside from the usual public relations set pieces, what good has the U.N. or its banks really done for Africans in sixty-five years? The reality is nothing really improves; things only manage to stay the same, or get worse.

The United Nations consists of more or less 150 member states. From this the U.N. claims to represent all the inhabitants of Earth. My question is, does it really? That is, does it actually represent any single individual on this planet? My answer would be no, not a one. The

U.N. represents only those who fund and steer it. One need only look at the U.N.'s stated agendas ("sustainable development", Agenda 21) to see just who it represents.

Etiological Implications

Because ETi reality has defied all the common myths put out by Hollywood, science fiction novelists, and ufology, there is need for some fresh thinking on this important subject. Worldviews change. Even the Catholic Church has recently made it known that it now accepts the possibility that intelligent extraterrestrial life may well exist, though I hasten to add that it still refuses to officially pardon the man who first posited that possibility, one Giordano Bruno. The Church officially "apologized" to *Galileo*, on October 31, 1992, but how do you apologize to someone you have burned at a stake?

In 1989, the International Academy of Astronautics (IAA) approved a SETI post-detection protocol developed by one of its committees. It was subsequently endorsed by the International Institute of Space Law (IISL), the Committee on Space Research (COSPAR) of the International Council for Science (ICSU), the International Astronomical Union (IAU) and the International Union of Radio Science (URSI). The protocol has little bearing on the reality, however. The chief reason for this is that it is a *SETI* protocol, not an ETi protocol, which means it contains *anthropic biases* and other preconceptions that simply do not apply.

A post-detection protocol will need to include and make special note of that most likely of scenarios, which it currently does not. I refer to the very contingency that has been enacted in front of us, namely: *we humans were discovered first.* Are we so sure of the superiority of our technologies that the notion seems impossible? We shouldn't be.

There is one item of politics that might be discussed by the United Nations now, though, I fear it may prove an intractable one. Both ETi and humans *should* have a common interest in preventing certain venal interests from setting the ETi-Earth scene and agenda. Unless I miss my mark, corrupt and self-serving motives and schemes will *not* ever apply here. It will not be "business as usual." Nor do I envision, for example, any *deals* of mutual enrichment being made. Intelligence agencies will not be allowed to make ETi interaction their private domain. There will be no secret collusions with military elites allowing them to dominate and otherwise have their way with the larger world -- not because I say this, but because ETi says it, or strongly implies it.

Where does ETi say this? In the passage that declared, simply, "Yes, Virginia, there *is* a right and a wrong." From this repeated signal alone, we should infer a very high standard of what is virtuous and seemly. For example: political slavery is wrong.

If the U.N. is serious about making contact with ethically advanced beings, it will need to make a choice. Freedom or tyranny. If authoritarian domination of all human life on this planet is really the U.N.'s ultimate goal, as it more or less states, then I don't think it need apply. It will also need to decide whether or not to acknowledge the ETi signals already made.

The "Declaration of Principles for Activities Following the Detection of Extraterrestrial Intelligence" assumes that those doing the declaring are intellectually capable of detecting a fully intelligent species. If detection cannot be made for lack of full *bicameral* functionality, or for the reason of plain arrogance and self-centeredness, fault cannot be attributed to those initiating the contact. ETi cannot be expected to demean or short-change itself by providing signals that any half-brain idiot could detect. We must allow that ETi will, as they say, have their pride.

Ah, but the bureaucratic machinery of the UN is a ponderous thing, one that moves slowly. Give it around fifteen years, though, and it tends to move, somewhere, by god. So with human reactions to events of 93/3 having taken their natural course these last twenty years, now seems as good a time as any to take things to the next level. What might be discussed by the U.N. in a post-933 world, is why any or all of this should be so. *Why* are we so...untouchable?

Dr. Stephen Hawking recently remarked in a documentary considering extraterrestrial life, "We only have to look at ourselves to see how intelligent life might develop into something we wouldn't want to meet." But who is "ourselves?" Is it the common man or is it the uncommon ruling man?

In this rather bleak vein, I find it odd that in a subsequent speech, Director Othman talked about how extraterrestrial affairs could become a topic for discussion at the UN, and made as an example the dangerous reality of Near-Earth objects (NEOs). She went on to say that should we ever hear from aliens, the world should have a coordinated response to that momentous occasion, arguing that "the UN is a ready-made mechanism for such coordination." It was a little bit like knocking on heaven's door, because it does not appear that the authors of Peekskill and SL9 are here to negotiate or establish formal relations with Earth at this time. We have some growing up to do first.

"The supranational sovereignty of an intellectual elite and world bankers is surely preferrable to the national auto-determination practiced for past centuries." - David Rockefeller

Fourteen
Deep waters

Let's dispense with unbelief and doubt and treat as a given the premise that a nonhuman sentience did, in fact, interface with our world. What does "not being alone" mean?

One thing we can say it means is that the Fermi paradox is obsolete, or needs to be modified somewhat. The question "where are they" need no longer be seriously asked, at least not in quite the same way. It turns out that we do not really need to know "where" they are, exactly, or where they come from, or what they look like. For now, it is quite enough to know that they exist. This does change things. Now we know we have an audience, or observers of our planet. This knowledge, this coming of cosmic age, means we must begin to put away those childish superstitious beliefs and behaviors that have animated our history for the last five to six thousand years, and face the real *universe,* to put our *best* face forward. This means a new paradigm and cosmological narrative are needed.

Another thing it means is that in large organized groups, anyway, we humans have not shown ourselves to be very fit company. It seems our so-called civilized manners preceed us. It means our problems are behavioral and this has resulted in what is essentially a communication embargo of our species. ETi now wants us to know that they have placed such an embargo, and want us to think about why the quincentennial activation of HRMS provided them a perfect opportunity to slightly modify the status quo.

For a long time we humans nourished the idea that we were alone and that the universe revolved around us. Recently we have come to realize that we might not be alone or at the center of anything. We look around and see this impossibly immense clockwork of spinning and pulsating objects obeying physical rules, but no sentient others. Yet we know extraterrestrials have to be there, somewhere. Then the universe literally threw us a curve (a hint!), but being self-centered and rule-bound, we didn't quite catch it. In love with our own right arm, one tattooed with the words "logical positivism," we consumed the cosmic memorandum (93/3) like so much eye candy. So the dispatcher filed the denouement away, perhaps under the heading, "as expected." ETi has probably seen this sort of thing before, and what they see is a half-brain, bicameral world careening on the edge of a kind of self-imposed oblivio n. Indeed, ETi made pointed mention of this by tieing their opening signals to the events of 9/11, or so it would seem.

Even now they watch as we turn inward and sink into a kind of scientific dictatorship, the newest wrinkle in the human pantheon of totalitarianism. They watch a secret cabal comprised of self-appointed and unelected technocrats and mega-banks attempt to take control of the world and everything in it, through debt, false flag propaganda, and overarching force. Transhumanism, sustainable development, global warming, biotech, and eugenics engineering have all become code words for world government and neo-feudalism - a "new mankind." People are now the seeing the signs of a sophisticated tyranny being unceremoniously rolled out, as fiat money morphs into fiat world government -- "change" that only yesterday was denied or laughed off as "conspiracy theory."

ETi sees it all. What's probably more, ETi has seen it all before -- planetary civilizations that measure up short and so balk at the great and mandatory challenges of space.

With the ideas of individual freedom and national sovereignty now under assault like never before, the foundations, think-tanks, and alphabet assemblies that claim to guide the world proclaim there are too many of us, and then systematically propound steps to address "the problem." So what happened to spreading out to the planets and the stars? What would happen to all the lizard-eyed environmental concern if we were to have "sustainable" habitats in space? That's where you need them. The problems of human expansion and resource depletion go away, that's what happens, for outer space has unlimited resources and space. But no, word has come down that space colonization is *not* to be a high public priority item; it is too hard and too expensive. Colonizing space is not only hard and expensive, it is quite impossible given how we spend our time and resources -- in endless war and other manufactured crises, on murder-a-minute entertainments (zombies & vampires now the fashion), and ball games. We can do better than this. What's more, we have to do better than this, because it's the only real way out of our dilemma.

ETi's communication was contained within, indeed, was all about, the *choices* made. Our choice is this: remain within the terrestrial envelope and slide into a new world order -- i.e. totalitarianism and economic bondage on a global scale, or break off and away to the stars.

Humankind is just that close to solving *all* of its survival and economic problems, but we fall short by a yard. We once managed to take a few small steps outside our terrestrial envelope and we found it no easy place to make a life. Yet, spreading our wings in this manner *is* the answer. Indeed, it is the one overarching imperative of any *intelligent* sentient lifeform -- to go where no man has gone before. The truth of this is elementary, even if the hows and where-with-alls at this point remain anything but elementary.

Perhaps the crowning achievement of the age of enlightenment was the codification of a system of governance that protected the individual from the tyranny of the rich, and even that of the majority. Although execution of its principles was far from perfect, the principles themselves *were* perfect. These core principles were individual rights, equality under law, and freedom of choice.

INDIVIDUAL RIGHTS

Only individuals have rights, not groups. Therefore, do not sacrifice the rights of any individual or minority for the alleged rights of groups.

EQUALITY UNDER LAW

To favor one class of citizens over others is not equality under law. Therefore, do not endorse any law that does not apply to all citizens equally.

FREEDOM OF CHOICE

The proper function of the state is to protect and defend, not to provide or "police" the world. Therefore, do not approve coercion for any purpose except to protect human life, liberty, or property.

Under this revolutionary system, each individual is allowed to flourish and self-actualize in her or her own way. This state of political affairs has until recently led to the greatest advancement and wealth per capita the world has ever seen.

Now there is a strong political trend to take the world backward away from these principles. The push today from the heights of power is toward deindustrialization (I have watched the greatest industrial power in the world reduced to a pitiful shell during my lifetime), micromanagement of the people by the Nanny state, and scientific technocracy -- all run by bankers and corporations. I have watched a democratic republic turn to social fascism, and a system of small representational government comprised of checks and balances become so corrupted that its founders would now find it unrecognizable. From the stink of this corruption a new kind of kingfish has emerged, and a very arrogant and dangerous one at that.

Time after time

George Washington once wrote: "Labor to keep alive in your breast that little spark of celestial fire, called conscience." As briefly mentioned in chapter four, one of the experimental purposes of the Peekskill overture will have almost certainly been that of feeling for a human conscience. It wasn't as if reflecting on our earliest American history wasn't something an American Quincentennial was *supposed* to oblige us to do.

Having a conscience involves that inner sense of what is right and wrong in one's conduct and manners. Having a conscience impels its owner toward "right" action, or causes one to feel guilty about something. I don't think it is incorrect to say that the scientists at Ames and JPL exhibited a complete lack of historical conscience, for Peekskill triggered no such pangs from their scientific souls, not even after I put the issue of Peekskill/SL9 before them. I think ETi knew all of this would be the case. I also think their "test" was made as much, if not more, for *our* edification as for theirs.

I'm sure it counted for something, though, that some in the lay public took the opportunity to protest Columbus and his legacy on that pan-hemispheric occasion. Even Pope John Paul II, the great Catholic moralist of the day was given reason to reflect a bit. He gave an open-air Mass on Sunday, October 11, at a new 10-story monument to the explorer, one constructed for the momentous occasion by the government of the Dominican Republic, the country where Columbus set up his main base of operations in the new world. The pontiff mentioned the excesses of Columbus and those who followed him and said the anniversary was an occasion to lament and seek pardon for the many offenses committed against the natives during their "evangelization," which process he praised -- as if colonization and evangelization were two mutually exclusive things.

Amerindians saw the day as one of mourning rather than celebration. Thousands gathered in cities all over South American to protest not only Columbus, but indian rights, many hundreds of them making journeys on foot from as far away as Alaska. Indian sit-ins blocked traffic in Ecuador and Columbia. Bombs damaged Spain's embassy in Chile, a Spanish bank in Peru, and statues of Queen Isabella and Columbus in Bolivia, Mexico and San Salvador.

**The Dogs of Vasco Nunez de Balboa
attacking the Indians**

On October 12, 1992, the "New York Times" recounted a few of the atrocities perpetrated against the Amerindian natives during Columbus's first two voyages. "Columbus and his men seized Caribbean women as sex slaves, sent attack dogs to maul naked indians, and disemboweled other natives who resisted conquest." The main subject of the article concerned revisions in history curriculums in New York City's public schools with respect to Columbus, changes that revealed the machinations of the power-mad explorer.

I vividly remember watching the more than one-hundred "tall ships" sail like relic ghosts up the Hudson river on that bright autumn afternoon. Having been so recently stunned by ETi's astounding *touch*, I was one made keenly aware of how extra-solar "others" might view us. I remember driving to the Hudson river near the new Jacob Javits Center, looking for buildings for sale during the pre-procession hours (among other things, I was a real estate broker at the time). I also remember not having a camera, an oversight I have learned to regret: almost no pictures can be found on the internet of those 100 tall ships sailing up the Hudson river that day. Search the word "quincentennial" or "HRMS" on Google these days and the great and wonderful Oz has no idea what you are talking about (in HRMS's case, you'll have to spell out the entire four-word name).

One question ran through my mind that day. How does ETi see us? Have we advanced *ethically* in 500 years since the advent of science and guns? Have we become the sort of species that an extraterrestrial could safely have something to do with? In some ways, I had to say yes to this, but in other more important ways, no. It must be observed that we have become, if anything, rather *more* deadly to our own and other kind(s) of life than ever.

More than 100 tall ships—many of them famous antiques – from around the world converged on New York City's Hudson River to celebrate the American Quincentennial (500th anniversary of America's discovery).

Modern science and technology has certainly made it easier for the war-mongers to "dispatch" larger and larger numbers of people.

Although our rulers don't do anything quite so obvious as burn people at the stake, or, as Aztec rulers did, rip their hearts out as sacrifices to *their* Gods, anymore, modern methods of *real politik,* money, and resource control are every bit as deadly. That same old human insanity continues to rear its ugly head in more or less continuous fashion. Have we learned *nothing* from history?

Is it really any wonder that our reverence for *logical positivism* and *moral relativism* made it rather difficult for us to know an "intelligent" signal when one fell on us? Any normal, nominally aware and rational person seeing the full panoply of circumstances and details infusing the Peekskill and Jupiter impact events has to know, in their gut, that something "other" transpired here.

Dr. Shoemaker used his gut, eyes, and brain in understanding that science will need to know a lot more about asteroids and comets before it can hope to prevent one from slamming into our tender planet. He knew that a meteor one hundred meters in diameter slamming into Earth will wipe out a city; one 1500 meters wide might take out a state, or at 5,500 meters a hemisphere. He may not have had any hard proof that giant meteors still pepper our planet on a regular basis, like the one that fell in Tungusta in 1908 that flattened several hundred square miles of Siberian forest and lit the night skies of Europe for a year. Before 93/3, he had the common sense to know that it might be important to *assume* that they do, anyway, just in case.

Deep waters

There is nothing quite like sitting before a raging wood fire in the early Spring. It is at times like these, with a loving dog's long moist snout reposed across one thigh, that thoughts of friendship caress the soul. Don't ask me to explain its source or to pin it down but there radiates from this interworld interface, this overture most select and advanced, an underlying sense of kinship and affinity toward our race. It is here that thoughts turn away from staggering details and niggling arguments. Perhaps it was an expression of concern from one intelligent lifeform to another, or merely that of wisdom to its youth. As I reflect on the *faux pas* so blithely committed by the federal juggernaut, I wonder if only America could have been so brazen, bereft and full of itself.

There is nothing new about things going bump in the night. Hey, stuff happens all the time, and it is the nature of human beings to attach intelligent meaning to phenomena that baffle or awe them. Sometimes we invent fanciful entities to explain them, like ghosts, god, Pan, elves, leprachauns, or Annunaki. But, no matter who calls them what, they all eventually get tossed into that lovely bin called the unknown, and once we have done this, we like to mostly forget them.

I would submit, however, that the phenomena discussed in this book are of a completely different order. That is, it seems a gross understatement to characterize a train of comets colliding with Jupiter as something that somewhat predictably went bump in the night. One reason for this is that *this* thing that went bump in the night exploded with the force of something like fifty million hydrogen bombs. This "whatever-it-was" created ejecta plumes on Jupiter the size of *Earth!* Suddenly, the mystery, hallucination or superstition becomes quite serious, not so easily dismissed. This time we need to be quite sure just what it is we're talking about here -- hallucination or something Other. Absolutely everything we know and are or wish to be could depend on it, especially in a universe as unknown as ours. Everything.

Oh, did I forget to mention it? The High Resolution Microwave Survey was shut down by December 1993. Senator Richard Bryan of Nevada spearheaded the shut down of the "expensive" project after only one year of operation. He and others in the Senate, like William Proxmire who awarded HRMS his Golden Fleece Award, succeeded where HRMS had apparently failed, for not a single intelligently produced microwave beep was detected up to that time. But the deed was considered done only after more than $65 million of the $100 million ten-year allotment had already been spent. The great bulk of the money had been spent on developing the sohphisticated technology with which to search for intelligent signals. So over the next nine years, the American taxpayer saved the whopping sum of about $3 million per year, or about one-half the cost of a single Patriot guided missile.

Nevada Senator Richard Bryan issued a press release dated September 22, 1993 which chided NASA: "As of today, millions have been spent and we have yet to bag a single little green fellow. Not a single martian has said 'take me to your leader,' and not a single flying saucer has applied for FAA approval." (See Appendix to read the full press release.) Yeah, right.

NASA slid its dime into the little slot, twisted the lever down a few times -- to the *right* -- and, wouldn't you know, nothing came rattling down, not one brightly colored alien.

Does this matter? Probably not. NASA was so far off track by this point how *could* it matter? What does matter is that there is now evidence, however circumstantial, that the universe is alive and kicking. It kicked *us* in the pants, anyway. Twice. Although we sense from their signals only the facade of ETi, we have been given some small tributaries of initial relationship on which we might sail. At present this is all, but we would be horribly remiss if we did not cast off lines and weigh anchor, for who knows where those tributaries might lead us!

The scientists at NASA-Ames and JPL were clearly out of their depth in attempting to penetrate the mystery of ETi existence. Not so for those of us with a more balanced and human perspective. As a species, we are like half-naked pilgrims adrift in a dangerously swelling cosmic sea, when suddenly is seen a strong and consistent light off our starboard bow. This is closely followed by a series of interconnected and synchronized flashings. Aha! a pattern! We are stupefied, put in our place, but then we laugh and applaud and ponder the enormity of what has serendipitously befallen us.

Whether or not this review of the relevant facts has the slightest chance of poking through to a politically correct world, this is my message in a bottle. The age in which these things happened recedes quickly now. I have tried to tell of a time, not so long ago, when nature lost all control and delivered a most allusive and intriguing muse to the awe and mystery of all. Maybe we'll hear its clarion call for some better action on our part, maybe we won't.

At the end of the day, it all happened pretty much the way you'd expect it would, not exactly maybe, but pretty much. This fork in the road, this cosmic threshold lies directly on the way to wherever it is we are going. We pass through this opening in the thickets in the way that infants will walk clean under a table, head in the air, and emerge triumphantly on the other side, only to suddenly realize that we are all grown up, and not quite so lonely as we were before.

APPENDIX I

News Bulletin

Richard Bryan

United States Senator

State of Nevada

103rd Congress

For Immediate Release

Contact: Jim Mulhall 202/224-6244

Date: September 22, 1993

BRYAN AMENDMENT PASSES TO CUT EXPENSIVE SEARCH FOR "MARTIANS"

GREAT MARTIAN CHASE TO END

Washington, D.C. --- The United States Senate agreed with Senator Richard Bryan (D-Nevada) today by voting by more than two to one to eliminate an expensive program to find intelligent life in outerspace. The Senate supported Bryan's position by a vote of 77 to 23.

"The Great Matian Chase may finally come to an end," Bryan said. "As of today , millions have been spent and we have yet to bag a single little green fellow. Not a single martian has said, 'take me to your leader,' and not a single flying saucer has supplied for FAA approval. It may be funny to some, except the punchline includes a 12.3 million dollar price tag to the taxpayer."

Bryan offered an amendment to the NASA appropriations bill today to eliminate $12.3 million in funding for NASA's program to search for life in outer space. Bryan successfully eliminated Senate funding for the program in 1992, when the Senate Commerce Committee voted 11 to 6 in favor of a Bryan amendment to cut funding for the program, and the full Senate approved the Bryan cut. To avoid the cut, NASA simply renamed the program from the original: Search for Extraterrestrial Intelligence (SETI) to "High Resolution Microwave Survey."

"This is a horrendous case of bureaucratic arrogance that somehow by simply renaming the program NASA can avoid the cut," Bryan said. "NASA wants to spend more than $100 million and they have got to get the message that this program doesn't make the final cut. This is a low priority and should be put on the shelf"

"I hope that the conference between the Senate and the House will see this vote as a clear vote of no confidence for this program," Bryan said.

NASA officials advocate that the program is designed to search and identify signs of intelligent life in outer space by analyzing radio waves bouncing around in space.

"I don't doubt that some scientists in NASA really believe this should be funded, but this is a question of priorities," Bryan said. "Only in Washington, D.C. is $100 million considered small change. This is a lot of money, and, frankly, I think this money could better be left unspent, which means we don't have to borrow as much and add to the debt. It really is that simple."

- 30 -

APPENDIX II

Merlin Productions[*]

FILMS OF ENCHANTMENT
MADE BY
THE WIZARDS OF TELEK
A DIVISION OF EARTHRISE STUDIOS

22 September 87
Thomas Nelson Hackney
75 Henry Street #29F
Brooklyn, NY 11201

Tom:

Your long and thoughtful letter of last May deserved response before now, but unusual letters ofttimes take unusual periods to answer. Since there was a novel to complete, a trip to Venezuela with flights through the Andes and down Corridor Diablo by Angel Falls, and dugout canoes down the Camainas into the Amazon, and then a screenplay to write in a great rush, about two hundred other things on hand, your letter could be permitted to incubate. The period is done (along with the novel and the screenplay and other things and the flying, although I have some balloon flights next week), incubation lies behind us, and here I am in response.

You were kind with many of your comments -- especially this business of "tell things the way they are, that is, without fabric softenes and apologies."

That comes from an intrinsic face-to-face with life's realism. If you break it all down to the most simplistic approach, which means sweeping away the horseshit and cobblestones and the ego-sustaining rush, it boils down to one element: We are all born to die. Period, man, BIG FAT PERIOD. That is why we are born and nothing will stave off that predestiny from the moment of birth. At least in this plane, this mode of existence, there's the brief flare of the biological match, and we're gone. So the next step is what to do between opening one's eyes and leaving behind forever the vehicle that carried our bodily plasma around while we're here, surviving only by dint of the odds of numbers. Its all a matter of what accident you avoid, or illness, or madman, or being in the right place at the right time rather than the wrong place at the wrong time. IT IS ALL ODDS. If you fly in a commercial airliner in this country, the odds against being killed are 34 million to one. That's better than the wildest lottery. But if you're in the particular hunk of metal that transforms itself at jet speeds into broken blazing wreckage, whatever you are in the way of dreams is the tiniest, instantly-gone wisp of smoke. Knowing that vulnerability, strangely, makes you much stronger IF YOU CAN DEAL WITH IT. If not, then you belong to the goblins and they'll feast on your frightened bones all your life.

Mayhap I was fortunate in having my main occupations in life -- businesswise, that is -- both flying and writing. I have a peculiar approach to honesty. Peculiar because damned few live it and hardly more understand it. We're infatuated with homilies, and one of those homilies is HONESTY IS THE BEST POLICY. Of all the self-smirking bullshit of pious hypocrites, that's one of the best.

My philosophy is that IF YOU"RE HONEST BECAUSE HONESTY IS THE BEST POLICY, THEN YOUR HONESTY IS CORRUPT. Go ahead; chew on it and have fun with that one.

Now, I fly. Many kinds of airplanes. With flying my honesty has nothing to do with policy but with survival. I can bullshit you and everybody else with lots of wonderful things about what a great and terrific and skilled pilot I am, but if I did do that (which, fortunately for the sanity of my friends, I don't), I WOULD NEVER DO IT TO MY AIRPLANE.

I can crap everybody but the machine I fly, BECAUSE IF I LIE TO MY AIRPLANE IT WILL KILL ME. That's why iron birds and me are such great friends. Man, talk about your absolute honesty.!

The same with writing. If I crap everybody out there with, Gee, ain't I f*cking terrific as a writer!, I'm back in the same boat. After slinging all that garbage everywhere I go home to face the typewriter. And what happens if I lie to the typewriter. Shit happens, man, and shit comes out and all my verbalizations amount to disgust and rejection.

So, living in slivers of reality where I accept absolute honesty, I become apparently hardshelled to the rest of the nonsense afflicting most humanity. The greatest fertilizer to get through life is the bullshit of self-deception. Look around you; the world teems with it. Some of us break free to a much greater extent than other, and we smile (albeit at times a bit wanly) at that original concept: WE ARE ALL BORN TO DIE.

Some time ago I really slipped away from most of the mainstream of life. I hate to think of myself as someone ensconsed in the low rolling hills of Florida as the equivalent of a Tibetan Curious trying to learn things while wanting more from the pleasurable aspects of life than a loincloth and thongs, but maybe that is it. For years now I have refused all writing honors. I used to win those things left and right and one day I woke up AND I GREW UP and said, what the hell? and turned down the rubber chicken courses and the self-effacing slush from people crowding around, mumuring and gushing, "Oh, gosh, you're wonderful." One day when I heard that I said, simply, "Yes."

Then I walked from the room and never went back. I yield to my ego with awards in accepting only those that deal with flying. A few years back when Silver Wings (all pilots who've earned wings) honored me as a Pioneer Aviator with words of praise I blush even now (and won't repeat here, although they gave it to me scratched in brass), I enjoyed getting <u>that</u> one. But when the White House invited me to receive a gold medal from the President as one of the two leading newsmen of the world who made the space age possible, I turned it down flat and never went. Along with their invitation was a dress code. F*ck <u>that</u>, man. I told them to make someone else -- preferably number 2 or 3 -- happy and give their medal elsewhere. (Of course, Dee Dee never forgave me. She said get the damned medal and let's at least melt it down into our jewelry, but, the trip wasn't worth it.)

Now to your letter. When you attribute to me the effort to establish a technically viable spacecraft and space station "a major reality," I fear you do so for the wrong reasons. I've gone into that horsepuck nonsense of "for the good of mankind." First, mankind don't give a shit and many of them are violently apposed to anything save their own interests .....

Look at something <u>my</u> way, Tom. It puts individuality in perspective and strips virtually all physical or technical accomplishment on a long lasting basis. Look at yourself. Now lift yourself in your mind to your ceiling. If you're alone (the one one you see looking down) you're smaller, baby. Put a dozen people in the room with you and you are just about not there. You're the beginning part of the vertical inhabitants of the ant hill. Now go up a hundred feet. If you're alone you're a sliver. If you're in a crowd <u>you are gone</u>. The individual who is Tom Hackney no longer exists to the eye. You are not discernable. You are but an idea or a memory and I'd like to see you measure that in a cup or capture it in a plastic bag, and now I want you to go higher. Pretty soon, my friend, all the biggest buildings are below visual resolution. Five billion people have vanished into the smooth surface of a world made smooth by distance. (Take the smoothest billiard ball and blow it up to the size of earth and its mountains are horrendous.)

Do you reach what I'm offering? The physical -- or the physicality -- of the spaceship and the space station are absolutely <u>nothing</u>. Assemblies of plastic and steel and chemicals are for shit. Use, application and continuing upstream with the dream and THAT IS ALL.

There always has been, there is now, there will always be ONE frontier and that is the mind. Oh sure, getting humanity off the earth and onto the worlds of many different suns absolutely must be a grim, frantic, frenzied, fanatic and nonstop goal, because at this stage in evolution we don't even know where the hell the mind is or how it works, and so long as man exists on the planets of one star he is never more than a stellar twitch away from nonexistence. Don't give it fancy names like chaos or obliteration or annihilation. That's more self-effacing bullshit to sound important. Nonexistence, baby; that's all. Not even a fart of cosmic memory.

So we've got to get onto the worlds of different stars and then give ourselves the time and the space and the effort to bring the mind into its proper development. No greater challenge, no greater reward, no greater power, no greater promise than that.

GET OFF THIS KICK OF IMMEDIATE TECHNICAL GOALS, FRIEND, OR YOU'LL BE TRAPPED. EVERYTHING THAT IS CRITICAL TODAY, TECHNOLOGICALLY ESPECIALLY, IS TOMORROW'S DUST. You'll get lost in the backwash and the turmoil unless you learn to separate and stand back. What lies between your ears makes a mockery of everything else. Hey, the only thing man ever <u>invented</u> (he found everything else) is God. Conscience, love, piety, patriotism, music; all of it ARE CURIOUS HUMAN INVENTIONS.

No musician ever became great because of the sounds he made. ITS THE PAUSES BETWEEN THE SOUNDS THAT MAKE A

GREAT MUSICIAN. Incredible, isn't it? Its the silence that creates the greatest music. ....

Look, there's this thing called telekinetics. Moving a physical object from a distance with mind power. I've been doing it for three years. Objects balanced on vertical pivots. Horizontal turning, but in another room that is sealed off from the outside, under test conditions (including no incandescent lights, vacuum chambers, 30 watts flourescent s only, no air movement, the room SEALED), and I look through tempered glass and I can turn anywhere from two to sixteen such targets from five, ten, twenty feet away, or through a TV scanner, or even from a photograph. Tell this to some scientists, they'll call you crazy or that I'm a liar or faking it. Fuck them. Even Randi and I got into it and I offered ten grand spot cash if I could NOT do it, and he hasn't been seen since.

My point is that I have no idea of what I'm doing or how I'm doing it, and I wouldn't recognize a thought wave if I fell over it. Its weak, confusing, spray-like, but what if I could identify the resonance or energy beam or frequency? I can't do that because I don't even understand it, but if I did I COULD AMPLIFY IT and then you're on the way to making the whole world yours (if you're dumb enough to want it).

Chew on these last two paragraphs. It doesn't matter if you believe me. Or anyone else. What I can do isn't proportional to ANYONE else's beliefs. But if we could amplify, and join minds that can do this ....and we can move and lift .... ah, what's that sound? It's your imagination revving up, Tom. Welcome to the real world of sane madness.

Martin Caidin

APPENDIX III

(From the index page of the author's former website, Etigrail II)

THIS IS ETIGRAIL II

On the 500th anniversary of Columbus's discovery of America, NASA began its first search for extra-terrestrials, a 10-year, 100 million dollar radio-astronomy project called the High Resolution Microwave Survey. How rich was that?

Hello, welcome to Earth Central! You are one of a very few to now be exposed to the extraordinary circumstances and details concerning what may be mankind's first substantive interface with entities beyond our world.

The 56 minute video below reveals and discusses museum-quality evidence of intelligent nonhuman activity in our solar system. Although ET's preemptive *response* to NASA's somewhat dubious symbolism was neither replicable nor acceptable in a scientific sense, this did not preclude reception on a human level; the events in question appear far too coherent and elegant to have been mere accidents of nature.

Through a series of historic and unprecedented impact events, human beings are afforded not only a glimpse into beings of superior nature and capability, but a unique and fascinating window into themselves.

The <u>Ames</u> Research Center led the High Resolution Microwave Survey with its "<u>Targeted</u> Search" for extra-terrestrials. Mankind's first major, federally funded search for ETI was commenced on America's Quincentennial (Oct. 12, 1992), which commemorated the *last* time humans discovered a 'new world' exactly 500 years earlier. (Hello!)

Something went down one clear autumn night in 1992. What that something was is not exactly clear. The Peekskill fireball event was in any case not only unprecedented in that it was the first meteor ever filmed and recovered, but it was the single most documented, filmed and publicized terrestrial meteor event in history. Around twenty video recordings were made as the "lime-green" bogey shot up the east coast of the United States at 7:49 pm on Friday, October 9, 1992. NASA was about to commence, on the American Quincentennial (Oct.12), or Monday, a 10-year radio-astronomy project to look for signs of extra-terretrial activity within a few hundred light-years of Earth.

The stage was set.

By way of the Peekskill fireball event, a large series of rather curious coincidences attended the great double-occasion. Any one of them could have snagged the conscious observer, leaving him or her looking for more. And there were, so many more! Sometimes when you look into the void, the void looks back into you. Come and see what those "coincidences" were, and how they all tell a story. Humans like stories, don't they?

Appendix IV

The ETi Grail describes a substantial number of articulate and often coincidental details observed from three impact events. Below is a list of thirty-two of these details or signals, choices that strongly suggest an intelligent designer for these events. What is important to understand about these individual items is how they relate to each other. Taken together they achieve a critical mass of evidence to support the theory that all three unprecedented impact events were designed and executed by an intelligent extra-solar being or beings.

1. The Peekskill fireball/meteor event, the most fully documented and publicized meteor event in history, occurred October 9, 1992, three days before NASA's quincentennial activation of the High Resolution Microwave Survey (HRMS), a ten-year radioastronomical project commissioned by the U.S. Congress to search for intelligent life or activity beyond the Earth.

2. The Peekskill fireball was observed by thousands up and down the Eastern United States at 7:49 p.m. EST. This timing made it possible for up to twenty video recordings to be made by spectators at high school football games, among other in six states. This provided investigating scientists with an unprecedented wealth of video data from which to determine a complete profile on the fireball in terms of its flightpath, radiant, speed, origin and orbit in space, to name a few.

3. The fireball's color was reported by numerous eyewitnesses to be lime-green. This particular color is consonant with human concepts and stereotypes of aliens.

4. The Peekskill fireball's 700 kilometer observed flight began in northern West Virginia and terminated in Peekskill, New York. This flightpath allowed Washington D.C. to have the longest and best viewing of the fireball. Since HRMS was a NASA project funded by the U.S. Congress, it appeared that the fireball's dispatcher selected this particular flightpath in order to get the attention of the project's progenitors.

5. The Peekskill fireball broke apart into more than seventy fragments after oscillating at 6 Hz when the fireball was at a parallel with Washington D.C., making for a fairly spectacular show for the capital city.

6. The Peekskill fireball was first seen by terrestrial observers in the north-western West Virginia. The birthplace of the SETI paradigm, and a major particpant in the HRMS project was the National Radio and Astronomy Observatory (NRAO) located in Green Bank, West Virginia, which is located on a precise parallel about 35 miles southeast of the fireball's visible starting point.

7. On the Peekskill fireball's date of occurrence, October 9, 1992, the annual Draconid meteor show was at its apex. The meteor was not a Draconid, however, but a *sporadic* (see Glossary). This implies that the Dispatcher wishes us to know that they are not "draconian" in general nature, at least not with respect to the inhabitants of Earth. This appears to contradict popular human and Hollywood depictions of aliens.

8. The Peekskill meteor fragment recovered shortly after it impacted hit the ground at an angle of 77 degrees. This particular number is commonly associated with the concept of luck, which is opposite of skill. The dichotomy seems to express the central issue or question

posed by the event. What occurred was caused by either random nature (luck) or intelligence (skill).

9. The Peekskill meteor impacted a parked 1980 Chevrolet in Peekskill, New York. This allowed its owner to sell both the meteorite and Chevrolet to collectors for a sizable sum. It also allowed scientists to confirm that the projectile was, in fact, a meteorite, to classify, study, and display it, and create a complete aerodynamic profile for the meteorite.

10. According to scientists who studied video films of the fireball, "never before has so much time-resolved dynamical detail ever been recorded for a fireball-meteorite event"; and, "these are the first motion pictures of a fireball from which a meteorite was recovered." In other words, before Peekskill, no meteoritic fireball had ever been both filmed *and* recovered.

11. The name given the fireball/meteorite event was Peekskill. From this we have the Peekskill meteor event, and the Peekskill meteorite. The words peek and *skill* seem to suggest intelligent causation for the event inasmuch as the meteor impacted rather precisely through the right-rear signal-light of a car.

12. The recovered meteorite, which measured 4" x 5" x 11", appears to have smashed through the right-rear signal-light of a car. On the other hand, the tail-light of a 1980 Chevrolet Malibu measures about 4-1/2" x 22". The marksmanship of the nonhuman aimer theorized appears extraordinarily true, if not perfect in this case. This precision seems to beg the question: was this the result of blind, random nature or consumate, nonhuman skill?

13. The chrome bumper beneath the perforated signal-light was not damaged by the impact, yet the signal-light itself was pulverized from one end to the other. The thin chrome accent just above the signal-light is only slightly damaged or bent in such a way that

it dips down to frame or segregate the the numbers "933" on the license plate. This, in addition to the fact that the right signal-light was destroyed (not the left) seems to direct an observer's attention to the three numbers highlighted.

14. A substantial number of highly germane meanings can be gleaned from the numbers highlighted on the impacted car's license plate. For example, from 9-33 we have the date of the Peekskill event (Oct. 9), which was 3 days before HRMS activation on Oct. 12, and 3 days before the American Quincentennial, which also occurred Oct. 12.

16. 93/3 -- 93 symbolizes the Astronomical Unit for Earth (i.e. 93 million miles), and Earth, the 3rd planet from the Sun. The A.U., the average distance between the Sun and Earth, is the basic unit of space measurement used by human astronomers.

17. 93/3 -- an abbreviation for March, 1993. This was the month and year that a very similar, if much larger, meteor-string was discovered, i.e. comet Shoemaker-Levy 9.

18. 93.3 -- an agebraic expression for the weight in pouinds of the Peekskill meteorite. The Precovered meteorite weight 12.4 kilograms, which rounds off to 27.3 pounds.

19. 933 -- 3 x 3 yields 9. 32 = 9. This mathematical relationship seems to point up the biogalctic or psychological effect of NASA's pairing of HRMS with the Columbian quincentennial (i.e. 500th anniversary of Christopher Columbus's discovery of the "new world"). The result seems to admonish NASA for its somewhat dubious or questionable publicity stunt, inasmuch as the two momentous human events celebrated yield more than the sum (3 + 3) yields much more than the sum of these parts. That is, 3 x 3 equals much more than 3 + 3.

20. 933 - 911. The three coordinated impact events of "933" seem to allude to the three coordinated impact events of 911. The truth

177

behind both event sequences were unbelievable or unacceptable or unreported to a majority of their human percipients. Both were major milestones of human history, events on which the nature and tenor of human history pivoted.

21. 93/3 -- According to astronomers, comet Shoemaker-Levy 9 split apart into fragments on July 7, 1992, which was 93 days or 3 months before the Peekskill meteor split apart into fragments. Thus, although it appeared at first that the Peekskill fireball augured Shoemaker-Levy 9's appearance in March, 1993, in this one sense Shoemaker-Levy 9 actually augured the Peekskill event. This reverse symmetry suggests an intelligent designer behind both events.

22. The recipient of the Peekskill meteorite, Michelle Knapp of Peekskill, New York, celebrated her 18th birthday on October 12, 1992. Among other things, this reinforced and emphasized the momentous date on which NASA commenced its search for intelligent alien life.

23. NASA's so-called Targeted Search for ETI (extraterrestrial intelligence) was conducted and managed by the Ames Research Center, a major research center of NASA located in Mountainview, California. ETi's *aim* at a precise *target* in Peekskill, New York is unmistakable evidence that ETi is speaking directly to the ETI investigators at NASA-Ames.

24. The target struck by the Peekskill meteorite was a car's *right* signal-light, not the left. This seems to provide an answer to NASA main operating hypothesis, namely: ET exists. To wit: *"Right*, Ames!"

25. During the two years that preceeded the Peekskill event (1990 and 1991), the U.S. Defense Department rolled out the Patriot Missile in Iraq. The Peekskill meteor/impact event seems to speak to, indeed mimic, this highly publicized and widely disseminated roll out. It was as if to say, "Here's a small peek at OUR skill, baby!" That Washington D.C. had the best seat in the house from which

to view the speeding fireball indicates that the U.S. Congress wasn't the only targeted percipient (tested) that night.

26. Comet Shoemaker-Levy 9 exploded on its target, Jupiter, with a combined force of approximately 6 million megatons of TNT, or about 600 times the Earth's total nuclear arsenal. It was the most energetic event ever witnessed in our solar system.

27. Shoemaker-Levy 9 consisted of 21 fragments, denoted A through W, with the letters I and O not used. This seems consonant with the perennial human idea of comets auguring future events, in this case the approaching 21st century.

28. A man in Princeton West Virginia shot himself in the right foot three times with three different pistols on the morning of Wednesday, October 7, 1992. This rather humorous impact event is probably unprecedented in the "500"-year history of guns.

29. The number of times the Princeton man shot himself in the right foot (3), seems to relate to the message key found on Michelle Knapp's impacted Chevrolet (933). The word "right" is also allusive to the right signal-light impacted by the Peekskill meteor two days later. The additional fact that the town in which the shootings occurred was Princeton alludes to Albert Einstein and his theories of relativity. The resulting idea, that of man "shooting himself in the foot" seems to point up a major human dilemma, namely our possible future use of nuclear weapons.

30. One of the most curious and amazing aspects of all three events was that they occurred under the human radar, or to be more accurate, at the human threshold. As far as can be proven, only one human being picked up on these signals.

31. The Peekskill fireball event occurred 21 months before the 21 fragments of Shoemaker-Levy 9 impacted Jupiter. Both meteor-

strings impacted the back side of their respective targets. Meteor trains are observed extremely rarely.

32. The car impacted by the Peekskill meteor was a 1980 Chevrolet Malibu. The main advertising slogan used by this car manufacturer for almost 100 years is simply the word "Genuine", as in "Genuine Chevrolet." Shortly after the impact occurred, Chevrolet began using the slogan "Like a rock!" in its advertising. This logo works well as a graphical representation of what results when a meteor squarely and precisely impacts a long and narrow signal-light.

33. The articulating details surrounding and informing The Peekskill, Jupiter and Princeton events were not close, they were perfect. The meteor didn't just hit a car, as the media reported, it surgically removed a car's right rear *signal*-light, leaving the surrounding chrome either pristine or largely intact; the color of the fireball wasn't just green, it was lime-green; the meteorite's weight wasn't 27.2 pounds, it was 27.3 pounds; there were not 12, 5, or 11 comet fragments in Shoemaker-Levy 9, there 21, and so on.

Glossary

Ames Research Center (ARC) - a major research center of NASA located in Moffit Field in California's Silicon Valley. Participated in the High Resolution Microwave Survey by directing the "Targeted Search."

anthropic principle (anthropic bias) - A principle that states knowledge about limitations of your data collection process affects what inferences you can draw from the data.

Apollo-Soyuz mission - the first joint U.S.–Soviet space flight, and the last flight of an Apollo spacecraft. Its primary purpose was as a symbol of the policy of détente that the two superpowers were pursuing at the time, and marked the end of the Space Race between them that began in 1957.

a posteriori - not existing in the mind prior to or independent of experience; from particular instances to a general principle or law.

a priori - from a general law to a particular instance; valid independently of observation; not based on prior study or ex amination.

Astronomical Unit (A.U.) - is a unit of distance equal to 92,955,807.273 miles, or approximately the mean Earth-Sun distance.

Bailey, Herbert - a long-time friend and associate of your author. Sometimes called The Father of the Vitamin Revolution, Herb was a medical journalist and author of <u>Vitamin E: Your key to a healthy heart</u> (Bantam, 1964), the first million selling book on the subject

181

of vitamins. He wrote two volumes on the history of the anti-cancer agent, krebiozen -- Krebiozen K - Key to cancer? (Putnam's Sons, 1956) and A Matter of Life and Death (G. P. Putnam's Sons, 1958). Among his other books are Vitamin E - for a Healthy Heart and a Longer Life (Carrol & Graf, 1993), E - The Essential Vitamin (Bantam, 1983), GH3 - Will it Keep you Young Longer?(Bantam, 1983).

Beckley, Timothy Green - aka "Mr. UFO." New York City's best-known publisher and promoter of UFO books, magazines and subject matter.

Billingham, John - Vice-chair of the SETI institute board of trustees since 1963. He is currently Senior Scientist of the SETI Institute located at the Ames Research Center.

Bruno, Giordano (1548-1600) - 16th century philosopher, mathematician, cosmologist, poet and priest who theorized that the stars are suns, and all this logically entails, including the necessary existence of extraterrestrials. One of the important figures in the history of Western thought, he anticipated the cosmos most believe in today.

Burnham, Forbes - born Feb. 20, 1923, Kitty, British Guiana—died Aug. 6, 1985, Georgetown, Guyana. Prime minister of Guyana (until 1966, British Guiana) from 1964 to 1980 and president from 1980 to 1985.

Caidin, Martin Von Strasser - worked with Werner von Braun on "Project Moon" to send a payload to the moon in 1956 (or was it '58?). Co-founded the American Astronautical Society; author of 79 fiction and nonfiction books and inumerable screenplays, e.g. Cyborg, which was adapted for the popular television show "The Six Million Dollar Man," Marooned, which was made into a major Hollywood film of the same name starring Gregory Peck, David Janssen, James Franciscus and Gene Hackman, and, your author's favorite, Exit Earth. Also a literary client of your author (see Appendix).

Copernicus, Nicholas (1473–1543) was a mathematician and astronomer who proposed that the sun was stationary in the center of the universe and the earth revolved around it. Author of the book <u>De revolutionibus orbium coelestium</u> (<u>On the Revolutions of the Celestial Spheres</u>), which presents that theory.

COPUOS (Committee on the Peaceful Uses of Outer Space) - Formally established by the United Nations in 1959 by 1472(XIV). The mission of COPUOS is to review the scope of international cooperation in peaceful uses of outer space, to devise programs and research in this field to be undertaken under United Nations auspices, to disseminate information on outer space matters, and to study legal problems arising from the exploration of outer space. COPUOS has two subcommittees, the Scientific and Technical Subcommittee, and the Legal Subcommittee.

corpus callosum - a band of deeply situated transverse white fibers uniting the two halves of the cerebrum in humans and other mammals. It is the single bridge between the two hemispheres of the cerebral cortex, which allow the left hemisphere, specializing in langage and logical functions, and the right hemisphere, specializing in nonverbal and intuitive functions, to exchange information.

Douglas, Sen. Paul H. - (March 26, 1892 – September 24, 1976) was an American politician and economist, and major political proponent of Krebiozen. A member of the Democratic Party, he served as a U.S. Senator from Illinois for eighteen years, from 1949 to 1967.

Draco - the Dragon, a northern circumpolar constellation between Ursa Major and Cepheus. Also, a late 7th-century b.c. Athenian statesman noted for the severity of his code of laws.

Draconids - any of several unrelated meteor showers whose radiants are in the constellation Draco.

Stevan Durovic, M.D. - Discoverer of Krebiozen (see Krebiozen)

ETI - hypothetical Extra-Terrestrial Intelligences that behave and communicate the way humans do, or the way professional SETI investigators want or expect them to.

ETi - this configuration (with small "i") is used to differentiate between the hypothetical aliens that NASA and others search for, and the real entities that made indirect contact beginning with the Peekskill fireball and impact event. SETI scientists do not search for ETi, i.e. extraterrestrials with an overarching intelligence.

Etigrail - the name of two websites (1999-2010) by the author. Etigrail (1999-2003) consisted of well over 100 web-pages, and Etigrail II (2009-2010), which consisted of as many as four webpages, but included eight video documentaries and slideshows, from 2 minutes to 57 minutes in length. "Etigrail" won a Juno award in 2001.

Etiology - any study of causes, causation, or causality, as in philosophy, biology, or physics.

FAO (Food and Agriculture Organization) - a specialised agency of the United Nations that leads international efforts to defeat hunger.

Fermi paradox - The apparent contradiction between high estimates of the probability of the existence of extraterrestrial civilizations and the lack of evidence for, or contact with, such civilizations.

Galileo Galilei (1564-1642) - Italian physicist, mathematcian, and astronomer who provided astronomical support for Copernicanism, that the Earth revolves around the Sun. Galileo has been called the "father of modern science."

Dr. Phillip Handler - President of the United States National Academy of Sciences for two terms from 1969 to 1981. He was also a recipient of the National Medal of Science.

Dr. Stephen Hawking - a British theoretical physicist, cosmologist, and author. Hawking was the Lucasian Professor of Mathematics at the University of Cambridge between 1979 and 2009. Subsequently, he became research director at the university's Centre for Theoretical Cosmology.

HRMS (High Resolution Microwave Survey) - A NASA SETI project to search for microwave signals coming from an extraterrestrial intelligence; consisting of two elements: an all-sky survey and a targeted search. A 10 millionfold increase in capability over the sum of all previous searches was utilized using high-performance data processing equipment known as the Multi-Channel Spectrum Analyzer (MCSA).

John P. Holdren - Science "czar" for the Obama administration. A follower of Dr. Eric Pianca. Author of <u>Ecoscience</u>.

Ivy, Dr. Andrew C, M.D., PhD. - Medical scientist with seven honorary doctorates; was a major scientific proponent of Krebiozen. Vice President of the University of Illinois and head of its medical school. An AMA Section Chairman for Pathology; later directed research on Krebiozen in the U.S. from 1951-1965. Author of over 1000 medical research papers. Was selected by the A.M.A. to represent the United States at the Nuremburg Medical Trials with respect to medical ethics.

Jet Propulsion Laboratory - a federally funded research and development center and NASA field center located in the San Gabriel Valley area of Los Angeles County, California. Participated in the High Resolution Microwave Survey by directing the "All Sky" survey.

John G. Gelinas & Associates - International public relations firm based in New York City with offices in London. It's president was a registered foreign agent representing the country of Guyana.

Keldysh, Dr. Mstislav - a key figure behind the Soviet space program; President of the USSR Academy of Sciences (1961–1975), three times Hero of Socialist Labor (1956, 1961, 1971), and fellow of the Royal Society of Edinburgh (1968).

Knapp, Michelle - original owner of the Peekskill meteorite, which impacted her parked 1980 Chevrolet, October 9, 1992 at 7:41 p.m.

Krebiozen - a non-toxic body chemical (a poly-liposaccharide) discovered and isolated by Yugoslavian medical researcher Dr. Stevan Durovic in 1949, in Argentina. Theorized to be a universal cell growth regulator, it was shown to be objectively effective in reversing advanced malignant tumors in over 70 percent of cases, banned from interstate commerce by the F.D.A. in 1964.

Lamont-Doherty Geological Observatory - a major research component of the Earth Institute at Columbia University, a collection of academic and research units within the university.

Levy, David - an amateur comet-hunter who co-discovered comet Shoemaker-Levy 9, which bears his name.

Moseley, James W. - Editor, publisher and "Supreme Commander" of the UFO newsletter, "Saucer Smear", published since 1954.

Mr. Murphy - a term for the idea that anything that can go wrong generally does go wrong sooner or later.

"MUFON UFO Journal" - Journal of the Mutual UFO Network.

NASA - The **National Aeronautics and Space Administration** is the agency of the United States government that is responsible for the nation's civilian space program and for aeronautics and aerospace research.

National Radio and Astronomy Observatory (NRAO) operates the world's most sensitive single-dish radio telescope. It also operates Very Large Array (VLA), an array of 27 radio telescopes that is among the most productive research tools in astronomy, and the Very Long Baseline Array (VLBA), an array of 10 radio telescopes.

"Nature" magazine - first published on 4 November 1869, this British science magazine and journal is ranked the world's most cited interdisciplinary scientific journal.

February 1994 (Vol. 367) "The orbit and atmospheric trajectory of the Peekskill meteorite from video records," by P. Brown, Z. Ceplecha, R.L. Hawkes, G. Wetherill, M. Beech, and K. Mossman

Neitzche, Friedrich - German philosopher of the late 19th century who challenged the foundations of Christianity and traditional morality.

Patriot missile - A surface-to-air missile (SAM) system used by the United States Army and several allied nations; developed and manufactured by the Raytheon Company.

Peekskill meteorite - a 27.3 pound (12.4 kg) meteorite identified as an H6 monomict breccia (Wlotzka, 1994) recovered in Peekskill, New York, October 9, 1992. The short films can be viewed on the World Wide Web by searching the term "Peekskill fireball video."

Dr. Eric Pianca - scientific darling of the modern eugenics movement.

Proxima Centauri - a red dwarf star about 4.2 light-years distant in the constellation of Centaurus.

Roswell (UFO) **incident** - a report of an object that crashed in the general vicinity of Roswell, New Mexico, in June or July 1947, allegedly an extra-terrestrial spacecraft and its alien occupants.

Salkin, Harold - a close friend of the author for many years known in UFOdom as "the man of a thousand notes" (not to be confused with "the man of a thousand slides", Antonio Huneeus, our friend). One of the earliest ufologists, Harold worked with Kenneth Arnold at NICAP in the 1950s. He interviewed A. Einstein once, and was a personal aid to Admiral MacArthur during WWII.

"Saucer Smear" - a membership only publication consisting mainly of the missives from a coterie of UFO researchers and enthusiasts. Considered the oldest on-going publication concerning UFOs, "Smear" was founded by James Moseley in 1954, and remains its "Supreme Commander."

SCUD - a tactical ballistic missile that was developed by the Soviet Union during the time of the Cold War. Also, a missile utilized by Saddam Hussein in 1990-1 to attack Israel and U.S. targets in Saudi Arabia. The name came from Western intelligence agencies.

semiotics (pragmatics) - the study of signs and symbols as elements of communicative behavior; the analysis of systems of communication, such as language or gestures. Related to *pragmatics:* in linguistics, the analysis of language in terms of the situational context within which utterances are made, including the knowledge and beliefs of the speaker and the relation between speaker and listener.

SETI (Search for Extra-terrestrial Intelligence) - The collective name for a number of activities that undertake to search for intelligent extraterrestrial life. SETI projects use scientific methods to search for intelligent life.

Shoemaker-Levy 9 - Comet formally designated D/1993 F2 that broke apart and collided with Jupiter in July 1994, providing the first direct observation of an extraterrestrial collision of Solar System objects.

Shoemaker, Drs. Eugene & Carol - Co-discovers of comet Shoemaker-Levy 9, along with amateur comet-hunter, David Levy. Eugene Shoemaker helped pioneer the field of astrogeology by founding the Astrogeology Research Program of the U.S. Geological Survey in 1961, and was its first director. He was prominently involved in the Lunar Ranger missions to the Moon, which showed that the Moon was covered with a wide size range of impact craters.

Sitchin, Zecharia - a popular American author of books proposing an explanation for human origins involving ancient astronauts. Sitchin attributes the creation of the ancient Sumerian culture, perhaps the world's earliest advanced civilization, to the Anunnaki, an alleged race of extraterrestrials from a planet beyond Neptune called Nibiru.

sporadic - A meteor which is not associated with one of the regularly recurring meteor showers or streams.

"UFO Universe" - an internationally circulated (US, Can, GB) magazine about UFOs edited by Timothy Green Beckley in the mid-to-late 1980s. Your author wrote a piece in the Sept. 1988 issue about Martin Caidin's many aerial encounters with UFOs.

UNOOSA (United Nations Office of Outer Space Affairs) - an organization of the General Assembly of the United Nations located in Vienna charged with implementing the Assembly's outer space-related policies. Its director since 1999 is Dr. Mazlan Othman.

WRAP (Water Reclamation Algae Production) - a process for continuous culture and harvest of microscopic algae under controlled conditions, most notably in the treatment of sewage and other waste water. In these processes, algae are grown in shallow ponds designed to permit maximum exposure of the surface to sunlight, in which nutients (usually wastes) are supplied.